Cookbook

Roz Denny

SIMON & SCHUSTER

A VIACOM COMPANY

First published in Great Britain by Simon and Schuster, 1999
A Viacom Company

Simon and Schuster Limited
Africa House
64-78 Kingsway
London WC2B 6SX

Weight Watchers and 1, 2, 3 Success 2000 are Trademarks of
Weight Watchers International, Inc. and used under its control by
Weight Watchers (U.K.) Ltd.

Design and typesetting: Jane Humphrey
Photography: Steve Baxter
Styling: Marian Price
Food preparation: Sara Buenfeld

Weight Watchers Publications Manager: Elizabeth Egan
Weight Watchers Publications Assistant: Celia Whiston

A CIP catalogue record is available from the British Library

ISBN 0 68484 050 2
Printed and bound in Singapore

Pictured on the front cover: (clockwise from top left) Plaice Rolls with
Quick Mushroom Sauce, page 44; Spanish Chicken Casserole, page 60;
Chinese Chicken Liver Stir-fry, page 83; Red Berry Flan, page 133
Pictured on the back cover: Mozzarella and Tomato Pizza Toasts, page
22; Steak with Herb Butter, page 77

Contents

Recipe Categories

These are Budget meals
Ideal for those of you on a budget or anyone trying to save a few pence.

These are Creative meals
Choose one of these recipes when you are entertaining or feel like trying something different.

These are Family meals
They are ideal for midweek suppers or for times when everyone wants some delicious and satisfying traditional fare.

These are Quick meals
Turn to these recipes after work or when you simply want to whip up a tasty meal in as little time as possible.

Recipe Notes

Egg size is medium, unless otherwise stated.
Fruit and vegetables are medium-sized, unless otherwise stated.
It is important to use proper measuring spoons, not cutlery, for spoon measures.
1 tablespoon = 15 ml; 1 teaspoon = 5 ml.
Dried herbs can be substituted for fresh ones, but the flavour may not always be as good. Halve the fresh-herb quantity stated in the recipe.

V shows the recipe is suitable for vegetarians

A new Millennium, a new way of eating and a new you!

Welcome to the **Weight Watchers 1, 2, 3 Success 2000™ Cookbook**, which we hope you will find as successful and useful in your life as the Weight Watchers Programme has been for thousands of people.

Lifestyles are changing constantly. Modern technology may free you up from dull chores but it does put the pressure on in other areas. Many more people juggle home and family commitments with demanding jobs. You may enjoy a good quality of life that includes entertaining, hobbies, days and nights out, sports and activities. You want to look good and feel fit and healthy. And why not? Life is for the living.

So with that in mind we have divided the recipes in this book into various categories to suit your personal situation. If you want a dinner in a dash, for example, look for the *Quick* category. End of the month, with only a few pounds to stretch? Try the *Budget* dishes. For filling, wholesome food to suit everyone, look up *Family* recipes. Want to try new and interesting recipes? Then try your hand at *Creative* ideas.

We know that you want food that's satisfying, healthy and most of all tasty. If you're in a hurry, why not try a portion of *Baked Bean Pilaff* (page 22) or *Pasta Bows with Garlic Spinach Sauce* (page 104) with a ready-made supermarket salad. In just 15 minutes you'll have a complete, satisfying meal to fill you up and keep hunger at bay. For those of you who are dieting on a budget, you'll find some imaginative ideas for basic ingredients in recipes such as *Lemony Mousse* (page 136). Family recipes like *Chinese Noodle Pot* (page 25) and *French Bread Pizzas* (page 116) are bound to go down well with the kids. And if you want to be a bit more adventurous, recipes like *Thai-Style Chicken Salad* (page 63) or *Citrus Fruit and Strawberry Terrine* (page 140) are sure to satisfy your creative urges.

1, 2, 3 Success 2000™

If you're a Member of Weight Watchers then you'll know that these categories are taken from the **1, 2, 3 Success 2000™** Programme. Based on various lifestyle themes, **1, 2, 3 Success 2000™** comes from the same family as our previous 1, 2, 3 Programmes. It works like this ...

When you join Weight Watchers, your Leader will tell you how many Points you have available each day. All the food you eat is worth a certain number of Points, according to how many Calories and how much saturated fat it contains. As you spend your allocation of Points, you'll start to become aware that food which is high in saturated fat uses up more of your Points. This will encourage you to cut down on fatty food and go for low-Point versions instead. Bonus Points for exercise will encourage you to get moving – each activity is worth a certain number of bonus Points and you can spend these on extra food if you wish!

As well as following these basic guidelines, ensure your diet is healthy by eating a good variety of foods. Trying the new recipes in this cookbook will help you to do that. For example, you could make a new recipe each week. At that rate, there are enough recipes in this book to keep you going for several years. It's also important to fill up on fresh fruit and vegetables. The Government health authorities recommend at least five portions a day. You'll find we've used lots of fruit and vegetables in these recipes. And if you're hungry, just add an extra serving of vegetables or salad to your plate. To help you get used to planning your meals, we have included two menu plans based on **1, 2, 3 Success 2000**™ for a whole day in each chapter; every menu plan incorporates a recipe from the relevant chapter. These menu plans are all 20 Points per day, suitable for women weighing 10–12 stone. If your weight is below 10 stone you will need to start your day with fewer Points. If you weigh over 12 stone or are a man or young person (aged over 10 and under 16), then you will be allowed to spend more Points a day.

Finally, do take a lively interest in food. We live in exciting times – air transport has meant that many exotic foods are becoming common-place in our stores now. So, as well as eating in a healthy way, experiment freely. Flavourings, herbs and spices from all over the world will keep for a long time in your store cupboard. A dash or two of these can turn an ordinary dish into an exciting new taste discovery. So if a new jar, pack or bottle catches your eye, pick it up and read the label. And when you see a new ingredient in a recipe – buy it and try it. Healthy eating can be very exciting.

Enjoy what you eat!

Soups

Chapter 1

There's nothing better than a warming soup to come home to on a chilly day. They are often so hearty and nutritious that they're a meal in themselves and for Weight Watchers this is good news since they are usually low in Points and fat content. Soups can be thickened in many ways without adding too many extra Points: just throw in some small pasta shapes, rice or pulses. It's all good for you and tastes fabulous. Soup is such a wonderful food, it's full of different tastes, textures and colours and is fun to make too!

If you don't want to use stock cubes and prefer home-made stock, which always gives the best flavour, make sure that you cool the home-made stock first and then scrape off the fat which solidifies on top. It won't lose any of the flavour and your waistline will only thank you.

Serves 4 — Points per serving ½ — Total Points 2½ — Calories per serving 100

1 onion, chopped

2 garlic cloves, crushed

1 small red pepper, de-seeded and chopped

2 teaspoons sunflower or olive oil

400 g (14 oz) canned chopped tomatoes

½ teaspoon dried marjoram

1.2 litres (2 pints) vegetable stock or
water

40 g (1½ oz) long-grain rice

1–2 tablespoons Worcestershire sauce

1 teaspoon sugar (optional)

salt and freshly ground black pepper

Tomato, Red Pepper and Rice Soup

Freezing recommended • Preparation time: 10 minutes + 30 minutes cooking. Everyone loves tomato soup. This recipe, which is even better if made ahead, has the additional delicious flavour of red pepper. To make it more filling, long-grain rice has been added. If you want to pep it up a little, add a few dashes of hot pepper sauce when you serve it.

1 Mix the onion, garlic and red pepper with the oil and 2 tablespoons of water in a saucepan. Heat until sizzling and then cover and cook gently for 10 minutes, without lifting the lid. Shake the pan occasionally during the cooking time.

2 When the vegetables are soft, add the tomatoes and marjoram and cook for another 2 minutes. Then pour in the stock or water, rice, sauce, sugar (if using) and seasoning.

3 Bring to the boil, stirring once or twice and then cover and simmer for 15 minutes. Serve hot.

Serves 4 — Points per serving 2 — Total Points 9 — Calories per serving 135

300 g (10½ oz) large potato, peeled and
chopped finely

1 large onion, chopped finely

1 tablespoon sunflower or olive oil

1 teaspoon dried mixed herbs

1 litre (1¾ pints) vegetable stock

300 ml (10 fl oz) skimmed milk

1 tablespoon light soy sauce

salt and freshly ground black pepper

Potato, Onion and Herb Soup

Freezing recommended • Preparation time: 15 minutes + 25 minutes cooking. Delicious with chunks of crusty wholemeal bread or crispbread.

1 Mix the potato and onion with the oil and place in a large saucepan. Add 3 tablespoons of water and heat until sizzling.

2 Cover and cook gently over a low heat for 10 minutes. Shake the pan occasionally as the vegetables cook but do not lift the lid until the end of the cooking time.

3 Stir in the herbs, stock, milk, soy sauce and seasoning to taste. Bring to the boil, then simmer, uncovered, for 15 minutes, stirring occasionally.

4 If you wish you can blend the soup in a food processor or blender to make it smooth. Or, you can strain the soup (reserving the liquid of course) and press down on the vegetables with a potato masher. You can also leave the soup as it is. Check the seasoning and serve.

	Points per serving 1½
Serves **4**	Total Points 6½
	Calories per serving 150

Indian Carrot and Lentil Soup

4 carrots, grated coarsely

1 onion, chopped finely

2 garlic cloves (optional)

1 tablespoon sunflower or olive oil

1 teaspoon mild curry powder

1.2 litres (2 pints) vegetable stock or water

6 tablespoons split red lentils

½ teaspoon dried thyme

2 tablespoons half-fat crème fraîche (optional)

salt and freshly ground black pepper

V Freezing recommended • **Preparation time: 10 minutes + 35 minutes cooking.** Carrots are nicely complemented by aromatic spices. To make this soup more wholesome, and to give some body to it, add split red lentils which are cheap and easy to buy. Serve topped with a tablespoon of low-fat plain yogurt per portion.

1 Mix the carrots and onion with the garlic and oil in a large saucepan with 3 tablespoons of water.

2 Heat until sizzling, then cover and cook on a very low heat for about 10 minutes until softened. Shake the pan occasionally but do not lift the lid.

3 Stir in the curry powder, cook for a minute then pour in the stock or water and mix in the lentils, thyme and seasoning.

4 Bring to the boil, then turn down to a simmer and cook for 15 minutes, stirring occasionally, until thickened. Serve hot with dollops of the crème fraîche on top, if you wish.

Variation: For extra nutrition, flavour and colour add a good handful of chopped fresh spinach leaves or a bunch of watercress, chopped, during the last couple of minutes of cooking.

Menu Plan

Breakfast		Lunch		Dinner	
Small glass fruit juice	*½ Point*	**Salmon and Sweetcorn Chowder**		Medium chicken breast,	
Small banana, sliced on to	*1 Point*	(1 serving) page 14	*3 Points*	cooked in	*2½ Points*
Medium slice toast	*1 Point*	Crusty bread roll	*2 Points*	150 g (5½ oz) Sweet & Sour Sauce	
1 teaspoon low-fat spread	*½ Point*	Apple	*½ Point*		*2 Points*
				4 tablespoons cooked rice	*3 Points*
				Side salad	*0 Points*
				Small can 210 g (7½ oz) apricots in	
				juice	*1 Point*
				Small tub low-fat plain yogurt	
					1½ Points

Throughout the day: ½ pint skimmed milk *1 Point*   **Treat:** Weight Watchers from Heinz fat-free Pineapple Yogurt *½ Point*

Points per serving 1
Total Points 3
Calories per serving 85

400 g (14 oz) cabbage, shredded

1 onion, chopped

2 celery sticks, chopped

1 carrot, grated coarsely

1 green pepper, de-seeded and sliced thinly

125 g (4½ oz) mushrooms, sliced thinly

2 tablespoons low-fat spread (40% fat)

1.5 litres (2¾ pints) vegetable stock or water

1 teaspoon dried mixed herbs

salt and freshly ground black pepper

Chunky Cabbage and Vegetable Soup

ⓥ **Freezing recommended** • **Preparation time: 10 minutes + 35 minutes cooking.** The best cabbage to use is a crinkly Savoy, but any firm white or green cabbage will do. Serve hot with crusty bread.

1 Put all the vegetables into a large saucepan with the low-fat spread and 300 ml (½ pint) of the stock or water. Heat until sizzling and then cover and cook for 10 minutes without lifting the lid.

2 Pour in the rest of the stock or water and add the herbs. Season to taste. Bring to the boil and then simmer, uncovered, for 15 minutes.

Cook's note: This soup tastes best if you make it the day before and allow the flavours to mature. It reheats well, so it will last for two or more meals and can easily be reheated in the microwave.

Variation: To make this soup more substantial, just before serving add a tablespoon of cooked lentils or 50 g (1¾ oz) chopped cooked chicken or lean ham and remember to count the extra Points.

Chunky Cabbage and Vegetable Soup
Salmon and Sweetcorn Chowder *(page 14)*

Serves 4	Points per serving 1
	Total Points 4
	Calories per serving 85

Thai Hot and Sour Chicken Soup

1 litre (1¾ pints) water

2 chicken stock cubes

2 teaspoons ginger purée

1 small onion or large shallot, sliced very thinly

1 stem of fresh lemon grass, sliced thinly, or grated zest of 1 lemon

3 dried kaffir lime leaves or 1 large bay leaf (optional)

½ teaspoon salt

1 large red chilli, sliced very thinly

125 g (4½ oz) cooked chicken breast, skinned and shredded into fine strips

125 g (4½ oz) button mushrooms, cut in half

200 g (7 oz) ready-prepared young spinach leaves

1 tablespoon fresh lime or lemon juice

1 tablespoon Thai fish sauce or light soy sauce

salt and freshly ground black pepper

Freezing not recommended • Preparation time: 5 minutes + 15 minutes cooking. The Thais have many light, spicy soups with vegetables and small chunks of meat or fish that can be quickly cooked together and look so beautiful and inviting. The lemon juice gives the soup a delicious tangy flavour.

1 First, make the stock. Put the water into a large saucepan and crumble in the stock cubes. Add the ginger, onion or shallot, lemon grass or lemon zest, lime leaves or bay leaf (if using) and salt. Add most of the chilli strips but reserve some for garnishing. Bring to the boil and then simmer for 10 minutes.

2 Strain through a sieve, discarding the vegetables and returning the stock to the pan. Bring back to the boil.

3 When the stock is boiling, add the chicken, mushrooms, spinach leaves and reserved chilli strips.

4 Cook for 5 minutes on a simmer and then add the lemon or lime juice and Thai fish sauce or soy sauce. Season to taste. Reheat briefly and then serve immediately.

Broccoli and Cauliflower Soup *(page 16)*
Thai Hot and Sour Chicken Soup

Menu Plan

Breakfast		Lunch		Dinner	
Small glass fruit juice	½ Point	Potato, Onion and Herb Soup		Medium beef steak 225 g (8 oz)	
Medium bowl 30 g (1¼ oz) cornflakes		(1 serving) page 8	2 Points		5 Points
	1½ Points	Hovis mini loaf	1 Point	Medium jacket potato	2½ Points
Granulated artificial sweetener		2 satsumas	½ Point	1 tablespoons low-calorie coleslaw	
(optional)					½ Point
¼ pint skimmed milk	½ Point			Mushrooms, tomatoes, onions	0 Points
				2 tablespoons peas	1 Point
				Cooking apple, stewed with granulated	
				sweetener	1 Point
				Mixed with 1 heaped tablespoon	
				raisins	1 Point

Throughout the day: ¾ pint skimmed milk *1½ Points*   **Treat:** Individual chocolate Swiss roll *1½ Points*

Serves **4**

Points per serving 3
Total Points 12½
Calories per serving 220

1 small onion, chopped

1 potato, peeled and chopped

1 celery stick or small green pepper,
    chopped

1 garlic clove, crushed or 1 teaspoon
    garlic purée

1 tablespoon low-fat spread

500 ml (18 fl oz) skimmed milk

500 ml (18 fl oz) fish or chicken stock

½ teaspoon dried thyme

175 g (6 oz) fillet of fresh salmon, skinned
    and cut into bite-sized chunks

50 g (1¾ oz) smoked salmon, chopped

200 g (7 oz) canned sweetcorn, undrained

salt and freshly ground black pepper

To serve:

1–2 tablespoons chopped fresh parsley
    (optional)

a good pinch or two of paprika or mild
    chilli powder (optional)

Salmon and Sweetcorn Chowder

Freezing not recommended • Preparation time: 5 minutes + 25 minutes cooking. This classic American soup becomes a little more special with fresh salmon fillet and a few smoked salmon trimmings.

1 Put the onion, potato, celery or green pepper and garlic into a large saucepan with the low-fat spread and 3 tablespoons of water.

2 When the pan begins to sizzle, cover and cook for about 5 minutes on a low heat until the vegetables have softened.

3 Stir in the milk, stock, thyme and seasoning to taste. Bring to the boil and then simmer gently for 15 minutes.

4 Add both the fresh and smoked salmon and the sweetcorn together with the can liquor. Return to a gentle simmer and cook for another 5 minutes. Serve sprinkled with chopped parsley and dusted with a little paprika or mild chilli powder (if using).

Serves **4**

Points per serving 3
Total Points 11
Calories per serving 205

1 onion, chopped

2 garlic cloves, crushed, or 2 teaspoons
    garlic purée

1 celery stick, sliced thinly

1 small carrot, chopped finely

1 tablespoon olive oil

4 sun-dried tomatoes, soaked in hot water,
    then drained and chopped

400 g (14 oz) canned chopped tomatoes

1 litre (1¾ pints) vegetable stock

1 teaspoon dried basil or 1 tablespoon
    chopped fresh basil

425 g (15 oz) canned borlotti or pinto or
    red kidney beans, drained

60 g (2 oz) small quick-cook pasta shapes
    or macaroni

salt and freshly ground black pepper

To serve:

1 tablespoon grated fresh parmesan
    cheese

2 tablespoons chopped fresh parsley
    (optional)

Tuscan Bean and Sun-dried Tomato Soup

Ⓥ **if vegetarian cheese is used • Freezing recommended • Preparation time: 5minutes + 25 minutes cooking.** This delicious soup with the sunny flavour of sun-dried tomato is a little taste of the Italian countryside.

1 Mix the onion, garlic, celery and carrot in a large saucepan with the olive oil and 3 tablespoons of water. Heat until sizzling, then cover and turn the heat down to very low. Cook for about 10 minutes, shaking the pan occasionally.

2 Add the sun-dried and canned tomatoes, stock and herbs.

3 Bring to the boil, then simmer for 10 minutes. Stir in the beans and pasta, return to the boil and cook for a further 5 minutes until the pasta is softened.

4 Check the seasoning and serve hot sprinkled lightly with the cheese and parsley (if using).

Tuscan Bean and Sun-dried Tomato Soup

Serves 4
Points per serving ½
Total Points 2
Calories per serving 65

Broccoli and Cauliflower Soup

250 g (9 oz) broccoli head, thick stalk removed and chopped into small pieces

½ small cauliflower, thick stalk removed and chopped into small pieces

1 small onion, chopped

500 ml (18 fl oz) skimmed milk

500 ml (18 fl oz) water

a pinch of dried mixed herbs

50 g (1¾ oz) low-fat garlic soft cheese (optional)

salt and freshly ground black pepper

V Freezing recommended • Preparation time: 10 minutes + 20 minutes cooking. Broccoli and cauliflower make wonderful cream soups since they don't need anything extra to thicken them. They are also very healthy because you don't need to cook them in any fat.

1 Put the broccoli and cauliflower into a saucepan with the onion, milk, water, herbs and seasoning.

2 Bring to the boil and then cover and simmer. Cook gently for 15 minutes without lifting the lid.

3 Strain the soup, reserving the liquor. Put the vegetables into a food processor or blender and blend until very smooth and creamy, scraping the sides of the processor or blender several times.

4 With the machine blades whirling, slowly pour the reserved liquor back into the purée and reheat to serve. Mix in the garlic soft cheese (if using) just before serving.

Cook's note: For the ultimate creamy texture, pour this soup through a sieve and rub the vegetables through with the back of a ladle. It's not necessary but it gives the illusion of a soup with added cream!

Weight Watchers note: If the optional cheese is used, the Points per serving will be 1.

Snacks
and Light Meals

Chapter

2

Don't think that you have to give up snacks just because you are trying to lose weight. Depending on what they are of course, snacks can be an integral part of a healthy, well-balanced diet. So here are plenty of ideas for something to munch on when you feel you want a little something extra between mealtimes or you just feel like a light meal. Bread, eggs and vegetables can all be turned into delicious and satisfying snacks as you will see in this chapter. Eggs have actually been called 'nature's convenience food'. Not only are they quick to prepare, they are also high in protein content and full of vitamins and minerals. But try not to eat too many since the yolk contains fat.

All of these recipes are quick to prepare and some of them will even taste similar to some of the snack foods you buy but of course these dishes are much lower in Points and Calories.

1 teaspoon olive or sunflower oil

100 g (3½ oz) button mushrooms, sliced
thinly

a small pinch of dried thyme

1 large egg

1 medium slice of wholemeal bread,
toasted

⅓ punnet of salad cress, snipped

salt and freshly ground black pepper

Mushrooms, Poached Egg and Cress

Ⓥ if free-range egg is used • Freezing not recommended
• **Preparation and cooking time: 10 minutes.** To reduce Points and Calories, do not butter the toast. If the eggs are softly cooked, the yolk will moisten the toast. You could however, spread it lightly with a little yeast extract, brown sauce or tomato ketchup.

1 Heat the oil in a small saucepan and stir in the mushrooms with the thyme plus 1 tablespoon of water. Stir quickly to cook and then season. When wilted, remove from the heat.

2 Poach the egg in an egg poacher as normal.

3 Spoon the mushrooms onto the toast, top with the egg and sprinkle the cress on top.

125 g (4½ oz) smoked haddock or
cod fillet

1 tomato, chopped

a pinch of dried oregano (optional)

1 large egg

salt and freshly ground black pepper

Smoked Fish with Poached Egg and Tomato

Ⓥ if free-range egg is used • Freezing not recommended
• **Preparation and cooking time: 15 minutes.** For the best flavour, buy free-range organic eggs or eggs laid by hens fed on a mixed grain diet.

1 Fill a small shallow pan with water to come about 2 cm (¾ inch) up the side of the pan. Bring to the boil and then lower the heat to a gentle simmer.

2 Slide in the fish and cook for about 5 minutes until just firm. Remove the fish from the water and drain on kitchen paper.

3 Meanwhile, mix the tomato with a pinch of oregano, if using, and season. Set aside.

4 Crack the egg into a cup and then slide it into the water which the fish was cooked in. Poach for about 3 to 4 minutes until the egg white is firm and the yolk is still soft. Remove the egg carefully from the water with a fish slice, place on top of the fish and grind some black pepper on top. Serve with the chopped tomato on the side.

150 g (5½ oz) canned baked beans
1 large egg
1 medium slice of wholemeal bread,
    toasted
a little brown sauce, to spread

Spicy Beans with Poached Egg

 if free-range egg is used • Freezing not recommended • Preparation and cooking time: 10 minutes. Poaching eggs is one of the healthiest and quickest ways of cooking eggs. It is possible to buy egg poachers now with non-stick cups, although you may find a quick spray with low-fat cooking spray will ensure they slide out effortlessly if the pan is quite new.

1 Heat the beans in a small saucepan or in the microwave. Poach the egg in an egg poacher as normal.

2 Spread the toasted slice with brown sauce and spoon over the beans. Top with the egg and serve.

a small handful of fresh parsley sprigs,
    without stalks
a large sprig of fresh oregano or marjoram
    (optional)
1 large salad onion, chopped
60 g (2¼ oz) oyster mushrooms, sliced
    thinly
1 teaspoon sunflower or olive oil
1 teaspoon low-fat soft cheese
low-fat spray, for cooking
2 eggs, beaten and seasoned
salt and freshly ground black pepper

Oyster Mushroom and Herb Omelette

if free-range eggs and vegetarian cheese are used • Freezing recommended • Preparation and cooking time: 15 minutes. It is easy to buy small packs of fresh herbs now and they make delicious, quick fillings. Sliced fresh tomatoes sprinkled with a little salt and thyme make a good side salad.

1 Snip the herb sprigs into small pieces. Mix with the chopped onion and set aside.

2 Stir the mushrooms with the oil and place in a small saucepan. Heat slowly until hot, adding 1 or 2 tablespoons of water as the pan begins to sizzle. Cook for a minute or two until the mushrooms start to soften. Season and mix in the herbs and low-fat soft cheese.

3 Meanwhile, heat a small non-stick omelette pan and spray lightly with the low-fat spray. Pour in the beaten eggs and cook over a medium heat until the sides start to set.

4 Then, using a spatula, pull the set egg away from the sides and allow the liquid egg to run underneath. When the mixture is half set, scatter over the mushroom filling. Continue cooking the egg until almost cooked.

5 Hold the pan over a warmed plate and fold the omelette in half. Then push the omelette out onto the plate and serve immediately.

3 eggs

½ teaspoon salt

2 teaspoons sunflower or olive oil

3 salad onions, chopped

1 large courgette, sliced thinly

200 g (7 oz) cold boiled potato, sliced thinly

3–4 large fresh basil leaves, shredded

1 tablespoon grated fresh parmesan cheese

freshly ground black pepper

Courgette and Basil Tortilla Omelette

 if free-range eggs and vegetarian cheese are used ● Freezing not recommended ● Preparation and cooking time: 20 minutes. Turn some left-over boiled potato and eggs into a special light meal with courgettes and a few leaves of fragrant fresh basil.

1 Beat the eggs with the salt and some pepper to flavour. Heat the oil in a medium-size non-stick frying-pan until hot and then quickly stir-fry the onions, courgette and sliced potato for about 3 minutes. Leave in the pan and spread out to form an even layer.

2 Now pour in the beaten egg, tipping the pan to make sure the egg covers the whole of the pan. Scatter over the shredded basil and grated cheese.

3 Cook over a gentle heat, without stirring, until the sides start to set, then carefully lift away the set egg to let runny egg slide underneath.

4 Continue to cook slowly until all the egg is lightly set. If you want a firm set top, preheat the grill and quickly hold the pan underneath it to cook the top.

5 Loosen the edges of the omelette and slide a palette knife under the centre. Cut it in half and shake the omelette onto two warmed plates to serve. You could also serve it cut into wedges.

3 eggs

1 tablespoon light soy sauce

2 good pinches of Chinese five-spice powder

100 g (3½ oz) peeled prawns, thawed if frozen

1 tomato, chopped

1 salad onion, chopped

1 tablespoon chopped fresh coriander

low-fat cooking spray

salt and freshly ground black pepper

Chinese-style Prawn Omelette

Freezing not recommended ● Preparation and cooking time: 15 minutes. A simple and colourful filling. Use Atlantic prawns for the best flavour and if they are frozen, thaw them well first.

1 Beat the eggs with the soy sauce, five-spice powder, and a little seasoning. Pat the prawns with kitchen paper if they are wet and then mix them with the chopped tomato, onion and coriander.

2 Heat a small non-stick frying-pan and when hot spray lightly with low-fat spray.

3 Pour in the eggs and cook the base. Using a spatula pull the egg away from the sides and allow the runny mixture to slide underneath and cook.

4 When the egg is lightly set all over, spoon over the prawn and tomato mixture. Slide a palette knife under the egg and fold the omelette over the filling. Cook for a minute or so to let the top set, then slide the omelette on to a warm plate. Cut in two halves and serve.

Chinese Scrambled Eggs on Muffins

2 eggs
¼ teaspoons light soy sauce
4 teaspoons sesame seed oil
1 English wholemeal muffin, split in half
low-fat cooking spray
1 small salad onion, chopped (optional)
a pinch of Chinese five-spice powder or
**   sesame seeds (optional)**
freshly ground black pepper

ⓥ **if free-range eggs are used** • **Freezing not recommended** • **Preparation and cooking time: 10 minutes.** This recipe gives a tasty twist to one of the most popular snacks.

1 Beat the eggs with the soy sauce, the sesame seed oil and pepper. Start to toast the muffin halves.

2 Heat a small non-stick saucepan and when hot, spray with the cooking spray.

3 Pour in the egg and allow to set lightly and then stir gently. When it is half set, add the chopped salad onion and continue cooking until the texture of the scrambled egg is how you like it.

4 Serve immediately on the toasted muffin halves and sprinkle with either the five-spice powder or sesame seeds, if using.

Variation: To save Points, you could also serve the eggs on a medium slice of wholemeal toast. Points per serving would be 4.

Hot Tomatoes on Pesto Ciabatta Toast

2 large ripe tomatoes
low-fat cooking spray
2 medium slices of ciabatta bread
1 tablespoon pesto sauce
salt and freshly ground black pepper

ⓥ **Freezing not recommended** • **Preparation and cooking time: 15 minutes.** Introduce an Italian flavour to your quick snack with the lightest smearing of pungent pesto, a jar of which you may well have lurking in your fridge or cupboard.

1 Slice the tomatoes in half across the middle and season. Heat a non-stick frying-pan and when hot, spray with cooking spray. Add the tomato halves, cut-side down. Cook for about 3 to 5 minutes until nicely browned but still whole. There is no need to turn them. Remove the pan from the heat but leave the tomatoes in the pan.

2 Toast both pieces of the ciabatta loaf and then spread each lightly with the pesto.

3 Slide the tomatoes on top of the toast, slightly slashing the tomatoes with a sharp knife. This will allow the juices to flow and flavour and soften the toast. Season to taste and serve.

Points per serving 4

Total Points 16½

Calories per serving 215

150 g (5½ oz) mozzarella, cut into small
    cubes

4 large tomatoes, chopped

2 teaspoon dried oregano or basil

a good pinch of garlic salt or 1 teaspoon
    garlic purée

8 black olives

4 medium slices of wholemeal bread

salt and freshly ground black pepper

Mozzarella and Tomato Pizza Toasts

Ⓥ if vegetarian cheese is used • Freezing not recommended
• Preparation time: 10 minutes. You can make mozzarella cheese go
further by cutting it into small cubes and mixing it with other ingredients.

1 Mix the cheese and tomatoes together with the dried herbs, garlic
salt or purée and olives.

2 Preheat a grill and toast one side of the bread slices. Divide the
mixture into 4 portions and place on the untoasted sides of the bread.
Season lightly.

3 Return to the grill and cook until the cheese starts to melt and the
tomatoes are hot. Serve immediately.

Serves 4

Points per serving 4

Total Points 17

Calories per serving 280

2 x 100 g (3½ oz) packs of cook-in-the-
    bag basmati rice or long-grain rice

2 teaspoons low-fat spread

1 onion, sliced

2 teaspoons garlic purée or 1 teaspoon
    garlic granules

1 teaspoon curry paste

400 g (14 oz) canned Weight Watchers
    from Heinz baked beans

150 g (5½ oz) low-fat plain yogurt

1 punnet of salad cress, snipped

salt and freshly ground black pepper

Baked Bean Pilaff

Ⓥ Freezing not recommended • Preparation time: 5 minutes + 30
minutes cooking. Spicy baked beans make a wonderfully tasty and
simple meal which is ready in a matter of minutes.

1 First, cook the bags of rice according to the pack instructions. This
should take about 12–15 minutes depending on the rice. Drain the rice
but leave in the bags until ready to serve.

2 Meanwhile, melt the low-fat spread in a small saucepan and then
gently sauté the onion with the garlic purée or granules for about 7
minutes, stirring occasionally until softened.

3 Mix in the curry paste, cook for a minute and then stir in the beans.
Bring to the boil and cook for 2 minutes. Season to taste.

4 Snip open the rice bags, mix with the beans and then serve on
warmed plates topped with dollops of yogurt and the cress.

Mozzarella and Tomato Pizza Toasts

Serves 4

Points per serving 3½
Total Points 14
Calories per serving 130

12 fish fingers
½ cucumber, halved lengthways and
     de-seeded
2 salad onions, chopped finely
1 tablespoon chopped fresh parsley
1 tablespoon chopped fresh mint (optional)
200 g (7 oz) very low-fat plain fromage
     frais or low-fat plain yogurt
1–2 good pinches of dried dill weed
     (optional)
1 lemon, quartered
salt and freshly ground black pepper

Fish Fingers with Quick Cucumber Sauce

Freezing not recommended • Preparation and cooking time: 15 minutes. Fish fingers may seem like children's food, but they make good wholesome snacks for adults too! Serve them with this easy cucumber sauce on the side as well as some salad leaves and chopped tomatoes.

1 Preheat the grill until hot and then cook the fish fingers according to the pack instructions.
2 Meanwhile, make the cucumber sauce. Grate the cucumber coarsely into a large bowl and then add the onions, parsley, mint, yogurt, dill and seasoning.
3 Serve the sauce with the grilled fish fingers accompanied by the lemon wedges.

Variation: If replacing the yogurt with very-low-fat plain fromage frais, add ½ a Point per serving.

Serves 2

Points per serving 3½
Total Points 6½
Calories per serving 245

¼ iceberg lettuce, shredded coarsely
6 cm (2½ inch) length cucumber, chopped
     or sliced
1 carrot, chopped
1–2 salad onions, chopped
1 punnet of salad cress, snipped or half a
     bunch of watercress
2 tablespoons fat-free salad dressing
200 g (7 oz) canned sweetcorn, drained
200 g (7 oz) canned red kidney beans,
     drained
50 g (1¾ oz) cooked ham
salt and freshly ground black pepper

Ham and Sweetcorn Salad Bowl

Freezing not recommended • Preparation time: 15 minutes. This salad is delicious with rye crispbread with sesame seeds.

1 Mix the lettuce with the cucumber, carrot, onions and cress. Season and toss with the dressing.
2 Add the drained sweetcorn, beans and chopped ham or bacon or eggs. Stir lightly to combine. Serve in two bowls.

Variation: If you replace the ham with 50 g (1¾ oz) cooked bacon or 2 hard-boiled eggs, peeled and quartered, add 1 Point per serving.

250 g (9 oz) Chinese-style egg noodles

200 g (7 oz) canned concentrated chicken or mushroom soup

125 g (4½ oz) button mushrooms, halved

1 medium cooked skinless, boneless chicken breast, chopped

200 g (7 oz) canned sweetcorn with mixed peppers, undrained

1–2 tablespoons light soy sauce

Chinese Noodle Pot

Freezing not recommended • Preparation and cooking time: 15 minutes. Chinese egg noodles are a god-send for anyone with a hungry family to feed. They are so easy to prepare and filling too.

1 Break the noodles up roughly and then place them in a large bowl. Cover with boiling water according to pack instructions. Leave for 4–5 minutes and then drain and set aside.

2 Dilute and heat the soup according to pack instructions in a medium-size saucepan. Bring to the boil and add the mushrooms, chicken, sweetcorn (with the can liquid) and soy sauce to taste.

3 Simmer for 2 minutes and then toss in the noodles. Reheat and serve.

35 g (1½ oz) lean back bacon rasher, trimmed of rind and fat

2 crisp lettuce leaves, shredded finely

a few watercress or rocket leaves (optional)

1 ripe tomato

1–2 teaspoons fat-free salad dressing

1 medium slice of wholemeal or brown bread

coarse grain mustard or brown sauce

a few slices of onion, to serve (optional)

salt and freshly ground black pepper

Open Bacon Sandwich

Freezing not recommended • Preparation time: 10 minutes. A bacon sandwich is one of the great joys in life.

1 Dry-fry the bacon rasher until cooked on both sides. This should take about 5 minutes in total. Let cool slightly and then cut into slices.

2 Mix the lettuce with the cress or rocket, if using. Mix with the tomato and dressing.

3 Toast the bread slice and spread with mustard or brown sauce. Spoon on the salad and then top with the bacon slices and onion, if using. Season and serve.

Menu Plan

Breakfast		Lunch		Dinner	
Medium portion 150 g (5½ oz) grape-fruit segments in juice	*1 Point*	Medium burger bun	*2 Points*	Oyster, Mushroom and Herb Omelette	
Small tub low-fat plain yogurt		Small beefburger	*3 Points*	(1 serving) page 19	*3½ Points*
	1½ Points	Mustard or ketchup if desired	*0 Points*	2 potato croquettes	*1 Point*
		Tomato and onion slices	*0 Points*	Mixed salad	*0 Points*
		Apple and orange	*1 Point*	Fat-free dressing	*0 Points*
				Small tub 210 g (3½ oz) low-fat fruit fromage frais	*2 Points*
				Small banana	*1 Point*

Throughout the day: ½ pint skimmed milk *1 Point*   **Treat:** Fruit scone *2½ Points*, 1 teaspoon low-fat spread *½ Point*

Serves 2 | Points per serving 6
Total Points 12½
Calories per serving 305

2 large wholemeal rolls

100 g (3½ oz) reduced-fat hummous

1 Little Gem lettuce, leaves separated

1 carrot, grated coarsely

2 salad onions, chopped

2 tomatoes, sliced

1 tablespoon sunflower seeds

1 tablespoon low-fat French dressing

salt and freshly ground black pepper

Hummous and Salad Sandwich

V **Freezing not recommended** • **Preparation time: 10 minutes**
Eating a low-fat lunch at work can be a challenge. The secret is to pack a healthy supply of crunchy salad vegetables and chunks of fruit to nibble on throughout the day. Enjoy some low-fat yogurt and fruit with these rolls and remember to add the Points.

1 Split the rolls in half and spread with the hummous. Tear the lettuce into bite-sized pieces.

2 Mix all the salad vegetables together along with the sunflower seeds. Season and then add the dressing. Divide between the two rolls.

3 Wrap tightly in clingfilm. This will keep fresh for 3–4 hours in a cool place.

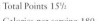

Serves 4 | Points per serving 4
Total Points 15½
Calories per serving 180

1 tablespoon sunflower oil

125 g (4½ oz) boneless, skinless chicken breast, chopped into small pieces

225 g (8 oz) chicken or turkey livers, thawed if frozen and chopped into small pieces

1 small onion, chopped

2 garlic cloves, chopped

2 teaspoon dried thyme

3 tablespoons dry sherry

2 teaspoon salt

3 tablespoons very-low-fat plain fromage frais

2 bay leaves

freshly ground black pepper

Country Chicken Pâté

Freezing recommended • **Preparation and cooking time: 20 minutes + chilling.** This simple pâté is excellent as a starter or light snack meal, served in small scoops with a medium slice of plain toasted wholemeal bread (1 Point) or Melba toast (6 small, thin slices are 1 Point).

1 Heat the oil in a small frying-pan and when hot, stir in the meats, onion, garlic and thyme.

2 Cook, stirring occasionally, for about 10 minutes until the meats are firm and the onion has softened.

3 Add the sherry and salt. Season with pepper and cook for another 2 minutes. Tip into a food processor or electric blender and whizz until smooth and creamy, occasionally scraping down the sides. Then blend in the fromage frais and whizz again to incorporate.

4 Spoon into a small bowl, level the top with the tip of a table knife and arrange the bay leaves on top. Chill until firm.

Quick Dips and Sticks

4 bread sticks (grissinni)

fresh vegetable crudités such as
cucumber, carrot, celery sticks,
radishes etc.

Ⓥ Freezing not recommended • Preparation time: 20 minutes
These two simple dips are ideal for those times when you feel peckish and should help to bridge the gap between meals.

1 To make the curry chutney dip, mix the onion, garlic purée and oil in a small saucepan and then heat until sizzling. Cover and cook over a low heat for 10 minutes, shaking the pan occasionally. Remove from the heat and cool. Put the mixture into a food processor or blender with the remaining ingredients for the dip and whizz until smooth.
2 Check the seasoning for both dips and then either serve immediately or store in the fridge for up to 2 or 3 days.

Curry Chutney Dip

Serves 4

Points per serving 2½
Total Points 9½
Calories per serving 110

1 small onion, chopped
1 teaspoon garlic purée
1 teaspoon sunflower oil
1 teaspoon mild curry powder
2 teaspoons mango chutney
200 g (7 oz) Greek-style plain yogurt
salt and freshly ground black pepper

Easy Tomato Salsa

Points per serving ½
Total Points 2
Calories per serving 35

200 g (7 oz) canned chopped tomatoes
grated zest and juice of 1 lemon
1 teaspoon garlic purée
1 tablespoon barbecue relish or
    Worcestershire sauce (optional)
2 tablespoons chopped fresh basil or
    parsley leaves
salt and freshly ground black pepper

Menu Plan

Breakfast		Lunch		Dinner	
Medium grapefruit	*1 Point*	**Chinese Scrambled Eggs on Muffins**		Medium fillet 120 g (4½ oz) smoked	
Medium slice toast	*1 Point*	(1 serving) page 21	*5½ Points*	haddock, topped with	*1 Point*
Spread with teaspoon low-fat spread		Sliced tomato and onions	*0 Points*	Poached egg	*1½ Points*
	½ Point	Small tub low fat-plain yogurt		Medium portion 200 g (7 oz) boiled	
			1½ Points	potatoes	*2 Points*
				Large portion 120 g (4½ oz) sweetcorn	
					½ Point
				Brussels sprouts, green beans	*0 Points*
				Pear	*1 Point*

Throughout the day: 1 pint skimmed milk *2 Points* **Treat:** Jam Tart *2½ Points*

Jacket Potatoes with Three Easy Fillings

4 x 200 g (7 oz) potatoes

salt and freshly ground black pepper

(V) **Corn and cheese filling if vegetarian cheese is used**

• **Freezing not recommended** • **Preparation and cooking time: 15 minutes.** Jacket potatoes were once considered a great treat because they took so long to bake, but now they can be done in minutes in the microwave. Because potatoes are a healthy food, they make a wholesome snack and are always popular with the family. Choose from three fillings below and serve with salad.

1 Wash the potatoes and pat dry. Cut a large cross on the top of each potato. Check your microwave oven instructions to see how long jacket potatoes should be cooked, making sure you allow sufficient time for cooking four potatoes at once.

2 Cook the potatoes according to the manufacturer's instructions and then allow them to rest for about 3 minutes.

3 Prepare your filling. Mix together the ingredients for any of the three choices below and season well. Heat the filling slightly, if desired. Cut a deep cross into each potato and then squeeze the potato from the base to open it up.

4 Use a table knife to make the opening even larger and spoon in the filling.

Weight Watcher's note: The Points for the potato add 2 Points per serving to each filling and add 8 Points to the total Points per recipe.

Baked Beans and Ham Filling

Serves 4

Points per serving 2
Total Points 9½
Calories per serving 270

400 g (14 oz) canned baked beans

2 tablespoons brown sauce

100 g (3½ oz) lean cooked ham, chopped

Corn and Cheese Filling

Points per serving 2
Total Points 8
Calories per serving 275

2 x 200 g canned creamed corn

100 g (3½ oz) half-fat Cheddar cheese, cut into small cubes

¼ teaspoon garlic powder

1 punnet of salad cress, snipped

Chicken Salad Filling

Points per serving 1½
Total Points 6
Calories per serving 245

2 medium cooked chicken breasts, skinned and chopped finely

2 salad onions, chopped

2 tomatoes, chopped

1 tablespoon low-fat mayonnaise

2 tablespoons low-fat plain yogurt

Tuna, Tomato and Cheesy Macaroni *(page 30)*
Jacket Potato with Baked Beans and Ham

Serves **2**

Points per serving 2
Total Points 4½
Calories per serving 150

2 teaspoons sunflower oil
150 g (5 oz) button mushrooms, sliced
    thinly
1 teaspoon mild curry powder
1 teaspoon garlic purée or a good pinch of
    garlic salt
2 teaspoons mango chutney
1 tablespoon low-fat plain yogurt
2 medium slices of wholemeal bread,
    toasted
a small pinch of dried mint (optional)
salt and freshly ground black pepper

Tikka Mushrooms on Toast

Ⓥ Freezing not recommended • Preparation and cooking time: 10 minutes. Mushrooms are delicious with curry.

1 Heat the oil in a small saucepan and stir in the mushrooms with a tablespoon of water. Cook, stirring for a minute or two until wilted, then mix in the curry powder, garlic purée or garlic salt.
2 Cover and cook for 2 to 3 minutes; then mix in the chutney. Reheat, season, remove from the heat. Stir in the yogurt. Spoon on to the toast.
3 Sprinkle the tops with dried mint, if using, or grind some more black pepper over the mushrooms and serve hot.

Serves **2**

Points per serving 6
Total Points 12
Calories per serving 225

1 Little Gem lettuce, torn into small pieces
1 carrot, grated coarsely
8 cm (3½-inch) long cucumber, sliced
    thinly
4 cherry tomatoes, halved
1 salad onion, chopped
4 rollmop herrings plus some of their
    vinegar dressing
a few slices of pickled beetroot
1 tablespoon chopped fresh parsley
    (optional)
salt and freshly ground black pepper

Rollmop Herrings with Salad

Freezing not recommended • Preparation time: 10 minutes.

1 Put the lettuce and carrot together in a bowl.
2 Stack the cucumber slices on top of each other and then cut into quarters. Add these to the bowl along with the tomato halves, chopped onion and seasoning.
3 Trickle over any liquor from the rollmops and toss the salad.
4 Arrange the rollmops on two plates accompanied by the salad and beetroot slices on the side. Scatter over the fresh parsley, if using.

Serves **4**

Points per serving 3
Total Points 12
Calories per serving 295

200 g (7 oz) short-cut macaroni
1 onion, chopped
100 g (3½ oz) sliced green beans
2 ripe tomatoes, chopped
½ teaspoon dried mixed herbs
200 g (7 oz) canned tuna in brine, drained
    and flaked
200 g (7 oz) cottage cheese with onions
    or chives
salt and freshly ground black pepper

Tuna, Tomato and Cheesy Macaroni

Freezing not recommended • Preparation and cooking time: 20 minutes. This is a low-fat version of macaroni cheese.

1 Boil the macaroni according to the pack instructions, adding the chopped onion to the water at the same time as the macaroni. Stir in the beans for the last 3 minutes of cooking time and then drain everything together.
2 Add the tomatoes and herbs as well as the tuna and the cottage cheese. Season to taste and reheat. Serve hot.

Salads

A salad is really just a great meal served cold! In other words, it is much more than a few salad leaves which will do nothing but leave you hungry. These salads are far from dull – they are full of flavour and sure to fill you up and leave you satisfied. Salads are very versatile and can really unleash your culinary creativity. They are also usually very quick which means you can also save your creative energy for things outside the kitchen. These recipes are ideal as light meals but they can also be doubled or trebled to serve as a side dish at a buffet.

When making a healthy salad, avoid adding dressings which have lots of oil and are therefore high in fat. The best thing to do is to use the special low-fat or even fat-free dressings which are now available in our supermarkets. And here are a couple of tips on how to improve the flavour of salads so you won't need to add as much dressing. If you are making a salad with boiled potatoes or any other starchy food, toss the ingredients while they are hot; this will intensify the flavour. Also, remember that cold food needs slightly more seasoning than hot food does, so add some more salt and pepper before serving if you need to.

Serves 4

Points per serving 2
Total Points 8½
Calories per serving 115

New Potato and Bacon Salad

500 g (1 lb 2 oz) new potatoes, washed or
    scrubbed

50 g (1¾ oz) lean bacon, sliced thinly

3 salad onions, chopped finely

2 tablespoons white wine vinegar or rice
    wine vinegar

1 teaspoon coarse-grain mustard

a small handful of fresh parsley sprigs,
    snipped roughly

salt and freshly ground black pepper

**Freezing not recommended • Preparation and cooking time: 20
minutes + cooling.** You'll get the best flavour by letting the potatoes
cool after dressing them with the bacon and onion.

1 Cut any potatoes which are large in half to make sure that all the
potatoes are about the same size. Then boil the potatoes in lightly
salted water until tender. Drain.

2 Meanwhile, dry-fry the bacon in a small non-stick frying-pan for
about 5 minutes, stirring until crisp. Mix the bacon with the salad
onions and then add the vinegar and mustard to make a dressing.

3 Toss the potatoes with the dressing and add the parsley. Season to
taste and serve at room temperature.

Serves 4

Points per serving ½
Total Points 2½
Calories per serving 75

Chinese Leaf Salad with Orange-Soy Dressing

200 g (7 oz) whole green beans, topped
    and tailed

2 head of Chinese leaf, torn into bite-sized
    pieces

2–3 celery sticks, sliced thinly

1 green pepper, de-seeded and sliced thinly

3 large salad onions, trimmed and cut into
    shreds

2 teaspoons sesame seeds

For the dressing:

juice of 1 orange

1 tablespoon white wine vinegar or rice
    wine vinegar

2 tablespoons soy sauce

1 teaspoon sesame seed oil

1 teaspoon clear honey

1 teaspoon garlic purée

1 teaspoon ginger purée

freshly ground black pepper

Ⓥ **Freezing not recommended • Preparation time: 15 minutes.**
Chinese leaf is a very versatile vegetable; you can eat it raw in salads or
lightly cooked as a vegetable. It also lasts a long time in the fridge so
you can easily use half of this recipe and then store the rest for later.
This salad is delicious with barbecued foods.

1 Boil the beans for 3 minutes in plenty of lightly salted water and
then drain and run under cold water. Pat dry with kitchen paper.

2 Mix the Chinese leaf with the beans, celery, pepper and salad onion
shreds. (The salad can be prepared up to this stage and then kept
chilled until ready to serve.)

3 Put all the dressing ingredients together into a screw-top jar and
shake well to blend. To serve, toss the dressing into the prepared leaves
and tip into a salad bowl. Scatter over the sesame seeds and serve.

New Potato and Bacon Salad

Chinese Leaf Salad with Orange-Soy Dressing

Mediterranean Tomato and Cucumber Salad

½ cucumber, cut in half lengthways, de-seeded and sliced thinly

4 large ripe tomatoes, quartered

½ small onion, chopped

a small handful of fresh parsley sprigs, snipped roughly

2–3 large fresh basil leaves, shredded, or a good pinch of dried mixed herbs

2 teaspoons olive oil

1 tablespoon fresh lemon juice

salt and freshly ground black pepper

 Freezing not recommended • Preparation time: 10 – 15 minutes + chilling. Bring a taste of sunshine to your table with this simple salad. Wonderful on its own as a quick starter or serve with some grilled chicken or fish for a light main meal. The tomato and cucumber make their own juices.

1 Place the cucumber in a colander and sprinkle lightly with salt. Leave to drain for 10–15 minutes. This helps to soften the cucumber and make it more moist.

2 Cut the cores out of the tomatoes and then slice the quarters again into wedges. Mix with the onion.

3 Add the parsley to the tomato and onion along with the basil or mixed herbs. Season with pepper and mix in the oil and lemon juice.

4 Pat the cucumber dry with kitchen paper and stir gently into the tomato salad. Chill lightly before serving if you have time.

Chicken, Edam and Sweet Pepper Salad

4 Little Gem lettuces, quartered

1 red pepper, de-seeded and cut into thin strips

1 bunch of watercress, stalks removed or a punnet of salad cress, snipped

10 cm (4-inch) length cucumber, sliced

2 medium cooked, boneless chicken breasts, skin and fat removed

1 tablespoon low-fat mayonnaise

2 tablespoons low-fat plain yogurt

2 tablespoons skimmed milk

½ small onion, grated

85 g (3 oz) Edam cheese slices

a good pinch of paprika or mild chilli powder

salt and freshly ground black pepper

Freezing not recommended • Preparation and cooking time: 10 minutes + chilling. All the family are bound to enjoy this colourful main meal salad.

1 Lay out the lettuce on a platter. Scatter over the strips of pepper and the cress.

2 Stack the cucumber slices on top of each other and then cut them into shreds. Add to the salad plate.

3 Pull the chicken into thin shreds with your fingers. Mix the mayonnaise with the yogurt, milk, grated onion and seasoning and then mix in the chicken.

4 Spoon this mixture on top of the salad. Cut the cheese slices into thin strips and arrange on top of the chicken. Finally, sprinkle with paprika or chilli powder. Serve lightly chilled.

Points per serving ½
Serves 2 Total points ½
Calories per serving 70

2 large carrots, grated coarsely

1 orange

1 tablespoon white wine vinegar

**2 tablespoons chopped fresh parsley or 2
salad onions, chopped finely**

**salt and coarsely ground or cracked black
pepper**

Spicy Carrot and Orange Salad

**Ⓥ Freezing not recommended • Preparation time: 10 minutes + 30
minutes standing.** Not only are raw carrots very healthy for you, they
are also a really cheap and tasty way to fill up a plate. Eat this as a
simple snack salad or serve it with a main course. No need to cook
even! To make it even healthier, add some sunflower seeds bought from
any health food shop or supermarket.

1 Place the carrots in a bowl. Season.
2 Squeeze the juice from the orange and mix with the vinegar. Toss
this dressing into the carrots along with the parsley or salad onions.
Allow to stand, if possible, for about half an hour before serving, to
allow the flavours to mingle.

Variation: Add some sunflower seeds to make this salad even healthier.
1 tablespoon is 1 Point.

Points per serving 2
Serves 2 Total points 3½
Calories per serving 130

**150 g (5½ oz) new potatoes, sliced
thickly**

2 small onions, chopped

1 tablespoon horseradish relish

**2 tablespoons very-low-fat fromage frais or
low-fat plain yogurt**

**100 g (3½ oz) canned tuna in brine,
drained and flaked into chunks**

**4 large crisp lettuce leaves e.g. Cos
lettuce**

4–6 large red radishes, halved

salt and freshly ground black pepper

Tuna and Potato Salad

**Freezing not recommended • Preparation and cooking time: 20
minutes.** Oily fish such as tuna can help our hearts to stay healthy so
it's a good idea to try to eat 2 small portions a week. Fortunately, most
oily fish is cheap and easy to buy.

1 Boil the potatoes until tender and then drain and cool.
2 Mix the onion with the horseradish and fromage frais or yogurt.
Gently combine this mixture with the potatoes and tuna, seasoning
lightly to taste.
3 Roll the lettuce leaves up and shred quite finely. Arrange these
shreds on two plates and spoon the salad on top. Dot with the radish
halves and serve.

Serves 4 Points per serving 3
Total Points 13
Calories per serving 200

Spicy Chicken Waldorf Salad

450 g (1 lb) chicken breasts, skinned, fat removed and cubed

2 celery sticks, sliced thinly

1 small onion or 3 salad onions, sliced thinly

1 red apple, unpeeled, cored and cubed

1 large carrot, grated coarsely

a few sprigs of fresh mint leaves (optional), snipped coarsely

a bag of ready-prepared mixed salad leaves

salt and freshly ground black pepper

For the dressing:

1 teaspoon garlic purée or ½ teaspoon garlic powder

1 teaspoon mild curry powder

juice of 1 small lemon or lime

1 tablespoon low-fat mayonnaise

150 g (5½ oz) low-fat plain yogurt

Freezing not recommended • Preparation and cooking time: 20 minutes. A main meal salad is perhaps one of the easiest dishes to prepare when you rush in from work. Serve with plain boiled new potatoes or microwaved baked potatoes.

1 Place the chicken cubes in a bowl with the celery, onion, apple and carrot. Season.

2 Add the mint leaves, if using, and toss in the bag of salad leaves, reserving any attractive or frilly ones for garnish if you wish.

3 Whisk all the dressing ingredients together in a bowl and then mix the dressing into the bowl of chicken and vegetables. Check the seasoning and serve.

Menu Plan

Breakfast		Lunch		Dinner	
Small glass fruit juice	½ *Point*	Medium corn on the cob	1 *Point*	Medium fresh tuna steak 100 g (3⅓oz)	
English muffin	2½ *Points*	2 teaspoons low-fat spread	1 *Point*		1½ *Points*
1 teaspoon low-fat spread	½ *Point*	**Home-made Coleslaw**		Medium portion 200 g (7 oz) boiled	
Heaped teaspoon jam or marmalade		(1 serving) page 40	½ *Point*	potatoes	2 *Points*
	½ *Point*	Mini pitta	1 *Point*	Large portion 120 g (4½ oz) sweetcorn	
		2 satsumas or tangerines	½ *Point*		½ *Point*
				Green beans, carrots	0 *Points*
				Small can (210 g) pineapple in juice	
					½ *Point*
				Small tub low-fat plain yogurt	
					1½ *Points*

Throughout the day: ½ pint skimmed milk *1 Point*   **Treat:** Small pot 110 g (4 oz) fruit trifle *5 Points*

Serves **4**

Points per serving 2
Total Points 7½
Calories per serving 260

2 teaspoons salt

200 g (7 oz) long-grain rice

3 tablespoons fat-free French dressing

2 salad onions, chopped

2 carrots, grated coarsely

200 g (7 oz) canned sweetcorn, drained

2 tomatoes, chopped

1 punnet of salad cress

salt and freshly ground black pepper

Easy Rice Salad

Ⓥ **Freezing not recommended** ● **Preparation and cooking time: 20 minutes + cooling.** A rice salad can be useful when you have friends around since you can make it ahead. A good basmati rice which will have a lovely natural flavour makes a rice salad much more interesting.

1 Add 2 teaspoons of salt to a large pan of water. Bring the water to a rolling boil and then carefully tip in the rice, stir once and then let the water come back to the boil.

2 Turn the heat down slightly and then cook the rice, uncovered, on a medium boil, for 12 minutes, just as you would potatoes. Drain the rice in a colander and rinse in cold water.

3 Tip the rice into a large bowl and toss it with the dressing. Season to taste. Allow to cool.

4 When the rice is cold, mix in all the vegetables, except the cress.

5 Spoon the salad onto a serving plate in a mound and scatter over the little salad cress leaves. Grind over a little pepper to serve.

Menu Plan

Breakfast		Lunch		Dinner	
Small glass fruit juice	½ *Point*	6 small thin Melba toasts	*1 Point*	New Potato and Bacon Salad	
Boiled egg	1½ *Points*	topped with Marmite and sliced		(1 serving) page 32	*2 Points*
Medium slice bread	*1 Point*	tomato	*0 Points*	Medium portion chicken Kiev	*8 Points*
1 teaspoon low-fat spread	½ *Point*	Small tub 210 g (4 oz) diet cottage		3 plums or apricots	½ *Point*
		cheese	1½ *Points*		
		Mixed salad	*0 Points*		
		2 satsumas	½ *Point*		

Throughout the day: 1 pint skimmed milk *2 Points*   **Treat:** Small glass wine *1 Point*

Serves **4**

Points per serving 3
Total Points 11
Calories per serving 155

250 g (9 oz) whole green beans, topped,
    tailed and halved
200 g (7 oz) canned red kidney beans,
    drained
400 g (14 oz) canned cannellini or borlotti
    or butter beans, drained
2 salad onions, or a small handful of fresh
    chives, chopped
3 tablespoons fat-free French dressing
a small handful of fresh parsley sprigs,
    snipped coarsely
50 g (1¾ oz) half-fat Cheddar, cubed or
    grated coarsely
salt and freshly ground black pepper

Three Bean and Cheese Salad

V **Freezing not recommended** ● **Preparation and cooking time: 15
minutes + chilling.** This is excellent as a side salad or a vegetarian
main meal.

1 Boil the green beans in lightly salted water for 3 minutes. Drain and
rinse in cold water. Cool slightly.

2 Mix the cooled green beans with the kidney beans and cannellini,
borlotti or butter beans. Toss in the salad onions or chopped chives and
the dressing.

3 Mix in the parsley sprigs and season to taste.

4 Spoon the salad into a serving dish and scatter over the cubed
cheese. Chill slightly and serve.

Serves **4**

Points per serving 4
Total Points 15½
Calories per serving 305

150 g (5½ oz) pasta shapes of your
    choice
2 tablespoons fat-free dressing
1 red or yellow pepper, de-seeded and
    sliced thinly
1 celery stick, sliced thinly
400 g (14 oz) canned chick-peas, drained
2 tomatoes, chopped
25 g (1 oz) snack-size peperami sausage,
    sliced very thinly
2 tablespoons soured cream
1 teaspoon garlic purée or 1 fat garlic
    clove, crushed
2 tablespoons chilli relish
a good pinch of dried oregano
1 tablespoon fresh lemon juice
salt and freshly ground black pepper
a few frilly lettuce leaves, to garnish
    (optional)

Mexican Pasta and
Pepper Salad

Freezing not recommended ● **Preparation and cooking time: 20
minutes + chilling.** This salad is very tasty and refreshing.

1 Cook the pasta shapes in plenty of lightly salted boiling water
according to the pack instructions. Then drain and toss in the fat-free
dressing. Leave to cool.

2 Mix the cooled pasta with the pepper, celery, chick-peas, tomatoes
and peperami.

3 Blend together the cream, garlic, chilli relish, oregano and lemon
juice and then toss into the salad. Season to taste. Chill slightly and
then serve on a platter lined with frilly lettuce leaves, if using.

Three Bean and Cheese Salad
Mexican Pasta and Pepper Salad

Points per serving ½
Total Points 2
Calories per serving 75

Home-made Coleslaw

500 g (1 lb 2 oz) white cabbage, quartered,
cored and shredded very finely

1 small red or white onion, sliced very
finely

1 celery stick, sliced finely

1 large carrot, grated coarsely

a good handful of fresh parsley,
chopped roughly

grated zest and juice of 1 small lemon

2 tablespoons low-fat mayonnaise or
creamy fat-free dressing

2 tablespoons skimmed milk

salt and freshly ground black pepper

 **Freezing not recommended • Preparation time: 15 minutes +
marinating.** Ready-made coleslaw is often drenched in a high-calorie
dressing and sometimes tastes rather sharp and artificial. The real thing
is easy to make and tastes much better. This recipe is also lower in
Points and Calories.

1 Place the cabbage shreds in a large bowl.
2 Toss the onion, celery and carrot into the bowl along with the
parsley, lemon zest and juice. Season.
3 Mix the mayonnaise or dressing with the milk and stir well into the
vegetables. They should only be coated lightly. Cover and leave in the
fridge to marinate for about 1 hour. Stir once before serving.

Serves 3
Points per serving 2
Total Points 6½
Calories per serving 165

Speedy Tuna Salad

200 g (7 oz) canned tuna in brine, drained
and flaked

a good pinch of dried thyme

2 salad onions, chopped or ½ small onion,
grated

1 tomato, chopped

200 g (7 oz) canned sweetcorn, drained

1 tablespoon low-fat mayonnaise

2 tablespoons low-fat plain yogurt or very
low-fat fromage frais

1–2 teaspoons chilli sauce or sweet
pickle

salt and freshly ground black pepper

**Freezing not recommended • Preparation time: 10 minutes +
chilling.** This salad can be used as a filling for pittas or rolls or mixed
with plain boiled rice, pasta or potatoes. It also makes a good filling for
baked potatoes.

1 Put the tuna in a large bowl with the thyme and then mix in the
salad onions or grated onion, tomato and sweetcorn.
2 Mix together the mayonnaise, yogurt or fromage frais and sauce or
pickle until smooth and then fold into the tuna mixture. Season and
chill until required.

Points per serving ½
Total Points 2½
Calories per serving 50

Marinated Mushrooms

200 g (7 oz) button mushrooms (plus a
few oyster and/or shiitake
mushrooms, if desired), sliced

1 small onion, sliced thinly

1 small carrot, cut into thin sticks

1 bay leaf

1 tablespoon olive or sunflower oil

juice of 1 lemon

1 teaspoon ground coriander

a small pinch of dried thyme

½ teaspoon salt

a small handful of chopped fresh parsley

freshly ground black pepper

V Freezing not recommended • Preparation time: 10 minutes +
marinating. Mushrooms are plentiful all the year round and make
excellent salads whatever the weather. This salad will keep in the fridge
for up to 3 days.

1 Slice the mushrooms. If using any shiitake mushrooms, remove the
tough stems first.

2 Put the onion, carrot sticks, bay leaf, oil, lemon juice, coriander,
thyme and salt into a medium-sized saucepan with about 5 tablespoons
of water. Bring to the boil, stirring, and then mix in the mushrooms.

3 Cover and cook gently for about 3 minutes and then tip into a bowl.
Allow to cool to room temperature to let the mushrooms marinate.

4 Chop the parsley sprigs roughly and add these to the mushrooms
too. Season to taste with the pepper and serve.

Points per serving 5
Total Points 20½
Calories per serving 360

Chicken Noodle Salad with Spicy Peanut Dressing

150 g (5½ oz) spaghetti, broken into 10
cm (4-inch) lengths

100 g (3½ oz) button mushrooms, sliced

2 x 250 g (9 oz) cooked chicken breasts,
skinned and shredded

3 salad onions, chopped

10 cm (4-inch) length cucumber, sliced

1 fresh red chilli, de-seeded and chopped
finely or ½ small red pepper,
de-seeded and chopped

salt and freshly ground black pepper

For the dressing:

1 tablespoon peanut butter

2 tablespoons light soy sauce

1 tablespoon white wine or rice wine
vinegar

4 tablespoons water

a good pinch of Chinese five-spice powder

Freezing not recommended • Preparation and cooking time: 10
minutes + cooling. This salad is bursting with freshness and spiciness.

1 Put all the dressing ingredients into a small saucepan and slowly
bring to the boil, stirring until smooth. Leave to cool.

2 Boil the spaghetti in salted water for 5 minutes or until just tender,
adding the mushrooms for the last minute or two so that they just
soften. Drain and toss with the dressing, then allow to cool.

3 Mix in the chicken and remaining vegetables, season and serve.

Serves 4 — Points per serving ½ — Total Points 1 — Calories per serving 20

½ cucumber

2 tablespoons chopped fresh mint

2 tablespoons chopped fresh parsley

4 tablespoons low-fat plain yogurt

a good pinch of ground cumin or mild curry
    powder

salt and freshly ground black pepper

Creamy Cucumber Salad

V **Freezing not recommended • Preparation time: 10 minutes + 30 minutes salting.** This is a very cheap and simple salad which is delicious as a starter salad served on a bed of lettuce or as a side dish with grilled fish or chicken breast. If you double the quantities, it also makes a good buffet salad.

1 Leave the skin on the cucumber and grate coarsely. Place in a sieve and sprinkle with a little salt. Leave to drain over a bowl for 20 minutes and then pat as dry as possible with kitchen paper.

2 Mix with the mint, parsley, yogurt, cumin or curry powder and black pepper. Check the seasoning and chill lightly before serving. If there is any excess liquid, drain it off.

Fish

4

Fish is true diet food; it's naturally healthy being high in proteins, vitamins and minerals and it's low in Points and Calories. White fish is very low in fat and even though fish such as tuna and mackerel are quite oily and therefore higher in Points and fat, they contain Omega 3 fatty acids, which are good for us because they contribute to a healthy heart. The only thing which can really make fish high in Points and Calories is what we do to it when we cook it; these recipes will help you to add lots of flavour and a minimum of Points.

Fish is also a versatile convenience food. It doesn't have to be cooked for long to make it tender. And you can buy it in so many different forms: fresh, frozen, canned, smoked and pickled. You can spend a little or a lot. It's up to you.

Fresh fish can be fun to experiment with so why not be adventurous and try some of the more unusual fish you see? They can be extremely delicious. Just ask your fishmonger to fillet and skin the fish for you, checking carefully for any stray bones when you get home. The best way to do this is to run your fingertips along the flesh and then pick out any bones you may find with some tweezers.

Points per serving 4

Total Points 15

Calories per serving 240

Salmon Grills with Honey-mustard Glaze

low-fat cooking spray (optional)

4 x 125 g (4½ oz) thick-cut salmon fillets
(ideally skinned)

2 teaspoons coarse-grain mustard

a pinch of dried dill weed (optional)

2 teaspoons clear honey

1 teaspoon lemon juice

1 lemon or lime, cut into wedges, to serve

salt and freshly ground black pepper

Freezing not recommended • Preparation and cooking time: 20 minutes. Salmon is such good value and is available all year round. Serve with a crunchy salad or the Creamy Cucumber Salad on page 42.

1 Preheat the grill until hot and then turn the heat down to medium hot. Lightly spray the grill rack with low-fat cooking spray, if desired. Season the fish fillets just before you cook them.

2 Grill for about 4 minutes on the skinned side. Turn over carefully using a fish slice. Grill on the other side for another 3 minutes.

3 Meanwhile, mix the mustard with the dill weed (if using), honey and lemon juice. Trickle this over the four fillets, season them with pepper and return to the grill for another minute or two or until the fish feels cooked. You can check this by pressing the top with the back of a fork. It should be firm and only just springy.

4 Remove from the grill and allow to stand for 3 minutes before serving accompanied by the lemon or lime wedges.

Points per serving 2½

Total Points 5

Calories per serving 170

Plaice Rolls with Quick Mushroom Sauce

2 x 150 g (5½ oz) large plaice fillets,
skinned

50 g (1¾ oz) button mushrooms, sliced

grated zest of 1 lemon

a good pinch of dried mixed herbs

150 g (5½ oz) canned Weight Watchers
from Heinz Mushroom Soup (or
½ x 285 g can)

a little chopped fresh parsley or chives
(optional)

salt and freshly ground black pepper

Freezing not recommended • Preparation and cooking time: 25 minutes. Plaice fillets are nice and plump and full of flavour. These rolls go well with creamy mashed potatoes and green beans.

1 Preheat the oven to Gas Mark 4/180°C/350°F. Check the fish for any fine pin bones and lightly season. Place the fillets in a small, shallow ovenproof dish.

2 To make the sauce, put the mushrooms into a small frying-pan with the lemon zest, herbs and the soup. Bring to the boil and cook quickly until softened. Remove the mushrooms with a slotted spoon.

3 Place the mushrooms on one side of the fillet and fold in half.

4 Pour the sauce over the fish. Cover with foil and bake for about 15 minutes or until the fish feels firm when pressed. Garnish with chives or parsley, if desired.

Salmon Grills with Honey-mustard Glaze
Plaice Rolls with Quick Mushroom Sauce

Chinese Stir-fry Prawns

250 g (9 oz) Chinese egg noodles
400 g (14 oz) frozen prawns, thawed
2 teaspoons cornflour
4 tablespoons light soy sauce
1 tablespoon sunflower oil
300 g (10½ oz) fresh, ready-prepared
  stir-fry vegetables
1 teaspoon sesame seed oil
2 teaspoons Worcestershire sauce
  (optional)
a good pinch of sugar
salt and freshly ground black pepper

Freezing not recommended • Preparation and cooking time: 20 minutes. Try to use North Atlantic prawns if you can – they have the best flavour.

1 Soak the noodles according to the pack instructions while you continue with the rest of the recipe. Drain and set aside.

2 Make sure the prawns are well thawed and then drain them in a colander. Pat them dry in kitchen paper and then mix in the cornflour and 2 tablespoons of the soy sauce. Leave to marinate for about 5 minutes.

3 Heat the oil in a wok and when almost smoking, add the prawns, stirring them quickly to heat them through. Toss in the mixed vegetables and continue stirring and tossing for 2 minutes.

4 Add the remaining soy sauce, the sesame seed oil, Worcestershire sauce, if using, sugar and a little seasoning. You probably won't need to add much salt. Serve with the noodles immediately.

Quick and Easy Fish Cakes

400 g (14 oz) white fish fillets, skinned
  and thawed if frozen
1 small onion, chopped
½ teaspoon salt
1 tablespoon light soy sauce
250 g (9 oz) potato, peeled and grated
  coarsely
1 tablespoon sunflower oil
freshly ground black pepper

Freezing recommended if fresh fish is used • Preparation and cooking time: 30 minutes. Enjoy these with some ketchup on the side.

1 Cut the fish into chunks and then place them in a food processor with the onion, salt, soy sauce and pepper to taste. Whizz to a thick purée but do not process too much.

2 Rinse the grated potato in cold water, then drain well and pat dry in a clean tea towel. Mix with the fish.

3 Using wet hands, shape into four large patties or 8 smaller ones. Make sure they are not too thick.

4 Heat the oil in a large non-stick frying-pan and cook the fish cakes over a medium heat for about 5–7 minutes on each side until they feel quite firm when pressed. Drain on kitchen paper.

Points per serving 2½
Total Points 10
Calories per serving 165

Oven-baked Cod with a Crispy Crust

low-fat cooking spray
600 g (1 lb 5 oz) cod fillet
3 medium slices of white or soft grain bread, crusts removed
a small handful of fresh parsley sprigs
1 small onion, quartered
½ teaspoon dried mixed herbs
grated zest and juice of 1 lemon
salt and freshly ground black pepper

Freezing not recommended ● Preparation time: 20 minutes + 30 minutes cooking. Serve with grilled tomatoes, peas and boiled potatoes.

1 Preheat the oven to Gas Mark 5/190°C/375°F. Spray a large, shallow roasting-pan with low-fat cooking spray.

2 Skin the cod fillet by running a large, sharp knife between the skin and flesh. (Or ask the fishmonger to do this for you before you buy the fish!)

3 Using a food processor, whizz the bread into fresh crumbs along with the parsley sprigs. Tip into a bowl. Add the onion to the processor and whizz to a purée.

4 Mix the onion with the breadcrumbs and add the herbs, lemon zest, juice and 2 teaspoons salt. Add black pepper to taste. The mixture should be quite moist. Lay the cod fillet in the roasting pan and then gently press the crumb mix on top.

5 Bake uncovered for about 20 minutes until the fish is cooked. (You can see if it is cooked by flaking the thickest part of the fillet with a fork and checking to see if it has cooked evenly). Take the fish out of the oven and allow it to rest for a few minutes before serving. Serve with the fish juices as a light 'gravy'.

Menu Plan

Breakfast		Lunch		Dinner	
Small glass fruit juice	½ Point	2 medium slices bread	2 Points	**Oven Baked Cod with a Crispy Crust**	
Medium bagel	3 Points	1 teaspoon low-fat spread	½ Point	(1 serving) above	2½ Points
Small low-fat cheese triangle	½ Point	Medium slice 45 g (1¾ oz) corned beef		Medium portion 200 g (7 oz) boiled	
Cucumber slices	0 Points		2 Points	potatoes	2 Points
		Onion and tomato rings	0 Points	Baby sweetcorn, carrots, mange-tout	
		Small tub low-fat plain yogurt			0 Points
			1½ Points	Apple	½ Point
		Medium portion 100 g (3½ oz) raspberries	½ Point		

Throughout the day: ½ pint skimmed milk *1 Point*   **Treat:** Currant bun, toasted *3 Points*, 1 teaspoon low-fat spread ½ *Point*

Curry-spiced Fish Grills

2 x 150 g (5 oz) cod fillets
2 teaspoons sunflower oil
1 teaspoon ground turmeric
1 teaspoon ground coriander
½ teaspoon ground cumin
¼ teaspoon mild chilli powder
freshly ground black pepper
a bag of speciality salad leaves, e.g. green
herb or Italian leaves
1 small lemon or lime, cut into wedges, to
serve
salt

Freezing not recommended • Preparation and cooking time: 20 minutes + 15 minutes marinating. You can use any fish for this recipe: cod, haddock, salmon, mackerel fillets or monkfish.

1 Check the fish for any pin bones.
2 Mix the oil with the spices and pepper and then pour into a polythene food bag. Add the fish and rub in the marinade well. Leave for up to 15 minutes in the fridge.
3 Meanwhile, preheat a grill or ridged grill pan until hot. Lay the fish on the rack or in the pan and season lightly with salt. Cook for about 5 minutes and then turn on to the other side.
4 Cook for a further 5 minutes or until the flesh feels firm when lightly pressed. Season again and serve on a bed of special salad leaves with lemon or lime wedges. The lemon or lime wedges should be squeezed over the fish just before eating.

Filo Prawn and Spinach Parcels

200 g (7 oz) young spinach leaves
200 g (7 oz) peeled prawns, thawed if
frozen
1 tablespoon low-fat mayonnaise
2 salad onions, chopped finely
1 tablespoon light soy sauce
1 tablespoon low-fat spread
8 sheets of filo pastry

Freezing not recommended • Preparation and cooking time: 40 minutes + 10 minutes cooling. Filo pastry is easy to use because it doesn't need to be rolled out. Just brush lightly with a little oil and water, fill and fold. Serve these parcels piping hot with salad or hot green vegetables.

1 Blanch the spinach in boiling water for just a minute then drain, rinse well in cold water and squeeze dry. Chop quite finely.
2 Pat the prawns dry and chop them. Then mix the prawns with the spinach, mayonnaise, onions and soy sauce.
3 Heat the low-fat spread gently with the water but do not allow to boil.
4 Brush one sheet of filo very lightly with the oil and water then place another sheet on top. Spoon a quarter of the filling at the top, fold in the sides, brush lightly with oil and water then roll up. Place join side down on a baking sheet.
5 Repeat with the remaining filo sheets, filling and oil and water until you have four parcels. Chill while you preheat the oven to Gas Mark 6/200°C/400°F.
6 Bake the filo parcels for about 20 minutes until golden brown and crisp. Cool in a wire tray for 10 minutes then serve warm and crisp.

Fish, Tomato and Leek Bake *(page 53)*
Filo Prawn and Spinach Parcels

Serves 2
Points per serving 3
Total Points 6½
Calories per serving 195

Chinese Baked Trout

**2 x 200 g (7 oz) trout, gutted but heads
    left on if desired**
1 salad onion, cut into thin shreds
1 small celery stick, cut into thin shreds
1 teaspoon ginger purée
2 tablespoons light soy sauce
1 tablespoon lemon juice
1 teaspoon clear honey
**some chopped fresh coriander or parsley,
    to serve**
freshly ground black pepper

Freezing not recommended • Preparation time: 15 minutes + 20 minutes cooking + 5 minutes resting. Trout are best when cooked simply with a few flavoursome ingredients, as they are in this recipe.

1 Slash the body of each fish twice on each side.
2 Lay each fish on a large sheet of foil and scatter the onion and celery shreds inside the body cavities. Mix the ginger, soy sauce, lemon juice, honey and some black pepper in a cup and then trickle over the two trout.
3 Wrap up the fish in the foil, seal well and place on a baking sheet. Leave to marinate while you preheat the oven to Gas Mark 5/190°C/375°F.
4 Bake for about 20 minutes until just firm. Remove from the oven and leave in the foil for 5 minutes. Then serve on the plates with the baking juices poured over garnished with coriander or parsley.

Cook's note: The fish head helps to hold the fish in shape as it cooks.

Chinese Stir-fry Prawns *(page 46)*
Chinese Baked Trout

Menu Plan

Breakfast		Lunch		Dinner	
Small glass fruit juice	½ Point	Medium pitta stuffed with lettuce and		**Chinese Stir-fry Prawns**	
Medium slice toast	1 Point		2½ Points	(1 serving) page 46	6 Points
Small can 200 g (7 oz) spaghetti in		Small can 100 g (3½ oz) tuna in brine,		Nectarine	½ Point
tomato sauce	2 Points	mixed with	1 Point	Small tub low-fat plain yogurt	
		Chopped onion and 1 tablespoon			1½ Points
		low-fat mayonnaise	1 Point		
		Baby tomatoes	0 Points		
		Large slice pineapple	½ Point		

Throughout the day: ½ pint skimmed milk *1 Point*   **Treat:** Jam Tart *2½ Points*

Serves **2**

Points per serving 2½

Total Points 5

Calories per serving 185

Old-fashioned Kipper Pâté

150 g (5½ oz) boneless kipper fillet

1 salad onion, chopped

1 tablespoon low-fat spread

2 tablespoons low-fat plain yogurt or
low-fat fromage frais

freshly squeezed lemon juice

freshly ground black pepper

a little freshly grated nutmeg

a small bay leaf, to garnish (optional)

Freezing recommended if used within 1 month • Preparation and cooking time: 15 minutes + chilling. It's a shame that kippers aren't as popular as they used to be; they have plenty of good fatty acids which contribute to a healthy diet and they're quite delicious.

1 Grill the kipper on the top side for only 5 minutes and then cool, skin and flake. Take out the large bones; the small feathery bones can be left and blended in.

2 Put the flaked fish into a food processor with the onion, low-fat spread, yogurt or fromage frais, lemon juice, pepper and nutmeg. Blend until smooth and creamy, scraping down the sides of the processor once or twice.

3 Spoon the mixture into a small serving bowl, smooth down the top and chill until required. Garnish with a bay leaf on top of the pâté if you wish.

Serves **4**

Points per serving 8

Total Points 31½

Calories per serving 555

Creole Fish Stew

600 g (1 lb 5 oz) fresh mackerel (one
large fish or two smaller ones), filleted
and skinned

1 tablespoon sunflower oil

1 onion, sliced thinly

1 red or green pepper, de-seeded and
sliced thinly

2 garlic cloves, crushed

1 teaspoon mild chilli powder

½ teaspoon ground cumin

1 teaspoon dried oregano

400 g (14 oz) canned chopped tomatoes

200 g (7 oz) long-grain American rice

salt and freshly ground black pepper

Freezing recommended • Preparation time: 10 minutes + 25 minutes cooking. One of the nice things about fish is it cooks quickly and always tastes tender. This stew is tasty with green beans.

1 Cut the fish into bite-size chunks.

2 In a large shallow pan, heat the oil and then sauté the onion, pepper and garlic for 5 minutes, stirring occasionally until softened. Add the chilli powder, cumin and oregano. Season and cook for a minute, then stir in the tomatoes.

3 Bring to the boil and simmer for 10 minutes. Meanwhile, cook the rice according to pack instructions, then drain, rinse in hot water and leave to stand in the colander.

4 When the sauce has finished simmering, drop in the fish and stir gently. Cook for a further 5 minutes until just firm. Serve the fish in the sauce with the rice.

Fish, Tomato and Leek Bake

2 leeks, sliced very thinly

2 large beef tomatoes, sliced thinly

2 courgettes, sliced

4 x 125 g (4½ oz) haddock or cod fillets
or steaks

juice of 1 orange

freshly squeezed lemon juice

1 vegetable or chicken stock cube

2 teaspoons dried mixed herbs

2 teaspoons low-fat spread, to dot

salt and freshly ground black pepper

Freezing not recommended ● Preparation time: 10 minutes + 25 minutes cooking. Serve with potatoes, rice or pasta.

1 Preheat the oven to Gas Mark 5/190°C/375°F. Blanch the leeks in a little boiling water for 2 minutes and then drain.

2 Scatter the leeks over the base of a shallow ovenproof dish and place the tomato and courgette slices on top. Season the vegetables and place the fish pieces on top of the vegetables.

3 Pour over the orange juice and lemon juice and then crumble over the stock cube and sprinkle with the herbs. Dot with the low-fat spread and then cover and bake for 20 minutes or until the fish feels just firm and the vegetables underneath are tender.

Pesto Fish with Tomato Pasta

125 g (4½ oz) pasta shapes (e.g. farfalle,
conchiglie, fusilli)

1 onion, sliced thinly

1 garlic clove, crushed, or 1 teaspoon
garlic purée

2 tablespoons dry white wine (optional)

200 g (7 oz) canned chopped tomatoes

a good pinch of dried marjoram

2 x 125 g (4½ oz) haddock fillets

2 teaspoons pesto sauce

salt and freshly ground black pepper

Freezing not recommended ● Preparation time: 10 minutes + 20 minutes cooking. Not many people realise how well pesto sauce complements fish, especially salmon and lightly smoked haddock.

1 Boil the pasta in plenty of boiling water according to the pack instructions. Drain and set aside.

2 Meanwhile, make the sauce. Put the onion, garlic, wine (if using), tomatoes, marjoram and seasoning into a small saucepan and simmer gently for 10 minutes.

3 Mix the sauce with the pasta. Preheat the grill to hot and lay the fish fillets on the grill rack. Season lightly and cook for about 4 minutes on each side. Spread the pesto sauce on the top of the fish a minute before it is cooked then return to the grill to seal. Serve the fish on top of the pasta.

Variation: Replace the smoked haddock with salmon and add 2 Points per serving.

Fish Pie

600 g (1 lb 5 oz) floury potatoes e.g. Cara, Estima, King Edwards, peeled and cut into large, even-size chunks

3 tablespoons hot skimmed milk

a little freshly grated nutmeg

500 ml (18 fl oz) skimmed milk

1 tablespoon low-fat spread

2 tablespoons flour

1 vegetable stock cube

½ teaspoon dried mixed herbs

300 g (10½ oz) cod fillet, skinned and cubed

300 g (10½ oz) smoked haddock fillet, skinned and cubed

125 g (4½ oz) frozen peas, thawed

2 tablespoons natural colour dried breadcrumbs

1 tomato, sliced

salt and freshly ground black pepper

Freezing recommended ● **Preparation and cooking time: 30 minutes + 25 minutes baking + 10 minutes standing.** This recipe for the popular family favourite has a quick and light white sauce so you can enjoy all the flavour without all the usual Points and Calories.

1 Boil the potatoes for 12–15 minutes until just tender. Drain and leave to dry in a colander for 5 minutes. Then mash the potatoes until smooth. (Do not use a food processor for this because the potatoes will go gluey.) Mix in the hot milk and nutmeg. Season to taste. Set aside.

2 Preheat the oven to Gas Mark 5/190°C/375°F. Put the 500 ml (18 fl oz) milk into a saucepan with the low-fat spread and flour. Bring slowly to the boil, whisking frequently until smooth and thickened. Crumble in the stock cube and mix in the herbs. Season to taste.

3 Drop the fish cubes into the sauce and mix in the peas. Then pour this into a shallow ovenproof pie dish. Spoon over the potatoes in dollops and then smooth them out with a fork so that they are level.

4 Sprinkle over the breadcrumbs and top with the tomato slices. Bake for 25 minutes or so until the top is golden brown and the sauce is bubbling up under the potato. Allow to stand for 10 minutes before serving.

Fish Pie

Fast Fish with Light Tartare Sauce

2 x 125 g (4½ oz) fillets of lemon sole or
    plaice, skinned

1 tablespoon capers, chopped very finely

2 small gherkins, chopped very finely

1 salad onion, chopped finely

1 tablespoon low-fat mayonnaise

1 tablespoon low-fat plain yogurt

1 tablespoon chopped fresh parsley

1 teaspoon olive oil

salt and freshly ground black pepper

1 lemon, sliced, to serve

Freezing not recommended • Preparation and cooking time: 20 minutes. If fish is cooked quickly at a high temperature with just a smidgen of oil, it tastes as if it has been fried. Serve with a low-fat version of tartare sauce.

1 Check the fish for any pin bones and then trim the edges. Cut each fillet in half lengthways so that you have four long, thin fillets.

2 To make the sauce, mix the capers, gherkins and onion with the mayonnaise, yogurt, parsley and seasoning. Set aside.

3 Heat a large, heavy-based, non-stick frying-pan and then heat the oil by brushing it quickly over the pan base using a rolled up sheet of kitchen paper.

4 Season the fillets lightly and then cook the best side of each fish first for 2 minutes until the flesh looks golden brown. Then carefully turn the fish over and cook the other side for 2–3 minutes.

5 Serve topped with the thinly sliced lemon and with a dollop of sauce on the side.

Tuna with Spicy Lentils

1 onion, chopped

2 garlic cloves, crushed

1 small green pepper, de-seeded and
    chopped (optional)

2 teaspoons sunflower or olive oil

400 g (14 oz) canned chopped tomatoes

1 teaspoon mild or hot chilli powder, to
    taste

1 teaspoon dried oregano or mixed herbs

400 g (14 oz) canned lentils, liquor
    reserved

300 ml (10 fl oz) water

1 vegetable stock cube, crumbled

100 g (3½ oz) short-cut macaroni

200 g (7 oz) canned tuna in brine, drained
    and flaked into chunks

salt and freshly ground black pepper

Freezing not recommended • Preparation time: 10 minutes + 20 minutes cooking. This is a great one-pot meal. Serve with chunks of crusty bread.

1 Put the onion, garlic, pepper (if using), oil and 2 tablespoons of water into a medium saucepan. Heat until sizzling and then turn the heat down, cover and cook gently for 5 minutes until softened.

2 Add all the other ingredients, including the liquor from the lentils, but not the tuna. Season and bring to the boil, stirring.

3 Turn down to a medium simmer and cook, uncovered, for 10 minutes. Stir in the tuna. Reheat for a minute or two and then serve.

Chicken
and Turkey

Chapter

5

Chicken and turkey were once quite a luxury, but now, thanks to modern rearing methods, they have become very affordable and form a regular part of our diets. This is good news because poultry is an excellent source of protein and without the skin, its fat content is lower than that of red meats. Whenever possible you should pull the skin off before cooking. Not only is poultry generally good value, it is also versatile and tends to be conveniently quick to cook. Most poultry today is sold as oven-ready or in pieces which are ready for grilling or casseroling. Breasts cook very quickly indeed, so be careful and don't overcook them. Thigh meat takes a little longer and is most suitable for stew dishes; since it marinates so well it is also ideal for spicy dishes. When buying a chicken or turkey, try to find free-range, organic or corn-fed birds; they have a much better flavour.

Serves 2

Points per serving 4
Total Points 8
Calories per serving 470

2 medium skinless, boneless chicken
   breasts
2 tablespoons soy sauce
1 teaspoon sesame seed oil
2 teaspoons ginger purée
1 leek, sliced very finely
1 carrot, cut into very thin sticks
125 g (4½ oz) long-grain rice, preferably
   Thai jasmine
100 g (3½ oz) fresh beansprouts
salt and freshly ground black pepper

Chinese Steamed Chicken

Freezing not recommended • Preparation and cooking time: 40 minutes + 5 minutes standing. Chinese steaming is a wonderful cooking method for Weight Watchers Members. It is easy, quick, light and above all very delicious! If you don't have a traditional Chinese bamboo steamer, now is a good time to buy one; they are cheap and easy to find. Otherwise, a metal steamer with a flat base will do fine, as long as you have a shallow heatproof dish that fits inside.

1 Cut the chicken into thin strips across the width of the chicken. Mix the soy sauce, sesame oil and ginger together in a large bowl and then mix in the chicken along with the leek and carrot.

2 Leave to marinate for 15 minutes while you boil the rice according to the pack instructions.

3 Put a large pan of water on to boil over which you can fit a bamboo or metal steamer. Find a heatproof dish which you can cook the chicken in and which will fit into the steamer.

4 Put the chicken, leek and carrot into the heatproof dish, adding any leftover marinade. Scatter over the beansprouts and seasoning.

5 Cover and bring the water in the pan underneath to a boil.

6 Steam for about 15 minutes, stirring the chicken once to separate it. The meat should be springy and firm when cooked. Leave to stand for 5 minutes before serving with the rice. You will find that there are some delicious natural juices from the chicken and vegetables in the dish, which can be trickled over the rice.

Chinese Steamed Chicken
Chilli Roasted Turkey Strips (page 72)

Points per serving 6
Total points 22½
Calories per serving 390

Quick and Easy Bean Cassoulet

1 teaspoon sunflower or olive oil

4 chicken quarters, skinned and separated into legs and thighs

1 large onion, sliced

2 garlic cloves, crushed

400 g (14 oz) canned chopped tomatoes

25 g (1 oz) mini snack-size peperami, sliced very thinly

300 ml (10 fl oz) chicken stock

½ teaspoon dried thyme

1 bay leaf

400 g (14 oz) canned cannellini or flageolet or pinto beans, drained

3 tablespoons natural colour breadcrumbs

salt and freshly ground black pepper

Freezing recommended • Preparation and cooking time: 45 minutes.
A cassoulet is a classic French dish from the southern city of Toulouse. Traditionally it is cooked with goose, spicy sausage and haricot beans, but this lighter version uses chicken, peperami and canned beans. Delicious with plain, boiled cabbage and a few boiled potatoes.

1 Heat the oil in a non-stick frying-pan (preferably one with a lid) and when hot, brown the chicken pieces quickly. Remove.

2 Add the onion and garlic to the pan together with 3 tablespoons of water. Bring to the boil, then cover and cook very gently until the onions have softened.

3 Add the tomatoes to the pan along with the peperami, stock, herbs and seasoning. Bring to the boil, return the chicken to the pan and then cover and simmer for 20 minutes.

4 Uncover and stir in the beans. Continue cooking for another 10 minutes. If using the breadcrumbs, preheat the grill.

5 Tip the chicken and vegetables into a shallow heatproof casserole and scatter over the crumbs, if using. Brown under a medium grill until lightly browned and crisp. Do not allow to burn.

Serves 4

Points per serving 4½
Total Points 17½
Calories per serving 260

Spanish Chicken Casserole

4 chicken quarters, skinned

2 teaspoons sunflower or olive oil

1 onion, sliced

1 green, red or yellow pepper, de-seeded and sliced

2 garlic cloves, crushed

2 teaspoons paprika

a good pinch of ground cinnamon

400 g (14 oz) canned chopped tomatoes

2 tablespoons dry sherry (optional)

150 ml (5 fl oz) chicken stock

juice of 1 small orange

8 stuffed olives, halved

salt and freshly ground black pepper

Freezing recommended • Preparation time: 15 minutes + 45 minutes cooking. This casserole is very easy to put together. Serve with rice or pasta.

1 Preheat the oven to Gas Mark 4/180°C/350°F. Heat a large non-stick frying-pan and when hot, brown the chicken quarters and then remove to an ovenproof casserole dish.

2 Add the oil to the frying-pan. When hot, stir in the onion, pepper and garlic plus 3 tablespoons of water. Cook for 5 minutes until softened.

3 Stir in the paprika and cinnamon, cook for a few minutes and then add the tomatoes, sherry (if using), stock, orange juice and olives. Season, bring to the boil and then pour the sauce over the chicken.

4 Cover and cook in the oven for 45 minutes until the meat is tender.

Quick and Easy Bean Cassoulet
Spanish Chicken Casserole

Serves 2

Points per serving 3½
Total Points 7
Calories per serving 250

¼ iceberg lettuce, torn into pieces

¼ cucumber, halved, de-seeded and sliced
   thinly

1 fresh red chilli, de-seeded and sliced
   thinly (optional)

a small handful of fresh coriander or flat
   parsley leaves, de-stalked

2 teaspoons sunflower oil

2 medium skinless, boneless chicken
   breasts, sliced into strips

1 small red onion, sliced very thinly or 2
   large salad onions, sliced

1 garlic clove, crushed

1 teaspoon ginger purée or ¼ teaspoon
   ground ginger

½ stem fresh lemon grass, sliced very
   thinly or grated zest of 1 small lemon

2 tablespoons Thai fish sauce or light
   soy sauce

Thai-style Chicken Salad

Freezing not recommended • Preparation and cooking time: 20 minutes. Thais love the combination of hot food and a cool salad. The contrast in temperature makes the food taste quite delicious and refreshing. You could also put some boiled Thai rice on the side.

1 Prepare the salad by placing the torn lettuce, cucumber, chilli slices (if using) and coriander or parsley leaves into a salad bowl.

2 Heat a large wok and when hot, add the oil and stir-fry the chicken strips for 2 minutes.

3 Add the sliced onion, garlic, ginger and lemon grass or lemon zest. Continue stir-frying for a further 2 minutes. Stir in the fish sauce or soy sauce and then toss everything into the salad. Eat immediately.

Serves 4

Points per serving 5
Total Points 21
Calories per serving 320

2 tablespoons light soy sauce

2 tablespoons barbecue relish or Chinese
   hoisin sauce

1 tablespoon tomato ketchup

1 teaspoon sesame oil

½ teaspoon onion or garlic powder

1 tablespoon Worcestershire sauce
   (optional)

150 g (5½ oz) low-fat plain yogurt

4 x 100 g (3½ oz) chicken drumsticks and
   4 x 75 g (2¾ oz) wing portions,
   trimmed of fat

salt and freshly ground black pepper

Spicy Chicken Drumsticks and Wings

Freezing not recommended • Preparation time: 15 minutes + 20 minutes cooking. These tasty chicken pieces can be baked in the oven, grilled or even barbecued if the weather is good.

1 Mix together the soy sauce, relish or hoisin sauce, ketchup, oil, garlic or onion powder and Worcestershire sauce, if using. Add the yogurt and season to taste.

2 Put the chicken and spicy mixture into a food bag and rub well together. Marinate for at least 10 minutes. Meanwhile, to ovenbake, preheat the oven to Gas Mark 4/180°C/350°F. If using the grill, preheat to medium heat. If barbecuing, heat the barbecue to medium heat.

3 To ovenbake, tip the chicken out into a roasting pan and bake for about 20 minutes, stirring occasionally until glossy and the meat is tender. If grilling, cook the chicken pieces under a medium heat for 15 – 20 minutes until tender, turning once or twice. If you prefer to barbecue, cook in the same way as you would if grilling.

Thai-style Chicken Salad
Spicy Chicken Drumsticks and Wings

Serves 2
Points per serving 6½
Total Points 13½
Calories per serving 675

Just-got-in Stir-fry

200 g (7 oz) Thai jasmine or long-grain rice

2 medium skinless, boneless chicken
    breasts, sliced thinly

1 tablespoon sunflower oil

1 leek, trimmed or 2 large salad onions,
    sliced very thinly

1 red pepper, de-seeded and sliced thinly

1 garlic clove, crushed, or 1 teaspoon
    garlic purée

1 teaspoon ginger purée (optional)

½ teaspoon Chinese five-spice powder
    (optional)

2 tablespoons dry sherry (optional)

2 tablespoons light soy sauce

1 teaspoon cornflour

1 teaspoon sesame seeds

salt and freshly ground black pepper

Freezing not recommended • Preparation and cooking time: 20 minutes. A stir-fry is the ideal meal to throw together after a long, hard day when you just want to relax with a filling and tasty dish. The optional ingredients aren't vital but they do give an authentic flavour.

1 Cook the rice according to the pack instructions. Meanwhile, heat a large wok or large non-stick frying-pan and when hot, toss in the sliced chicken with half the oil. Stir-fry for 2 minutes and then remove.

2 Add the remaining oil and when hot, stir-fry the leek or salad onions, pepper, garlic, ginger, if using, and five-spice powder, if using, for 2 minutes. Return the chicken to the pan.

3 Mix in the sherry, if using, with the soy sauce and cornflour plus 2 tablespoons of water. Stir this mixture into the wok, season and serve, sprinkled with the sesame seeds accompanied by the rice.

Serves 4
Points per serving 7½
Total Points 29½
Calories per serving 405

Chicken, Leek and Potato Pie

8 medium skinless, boneless chicken
    thighs, trimmed of fat and cubed

2 leeks, sliced thinly

2 carrots, peeled and sliced thinly

2 teaspoons low-fat spread

2 tablespoons flour

450 ml (16 fl oz) chicken stock

½ teaspoon dried mixed herbs

500 g (1 lb 2 oz) floury potatoes, scrubbed
    and sliced very thinly

1 teaspoon sunflower or olive oil

salt and freshly ground black pepper

Freezing recommended • Preparation time: 30 minutes + 30 minutes cooking. Ideal for all the family.

1 Heat a non-stick saucepan and when quite hot, brown the chicken quickly, then remove with a slotted spoon.

2 Add the sliced leeks, carrots, low-fat spread and 3 tablespoons of water. Stir well and when the contents start to sizzle, turn the heat down. Cover and cook for 5 minutes until the vegetables are softened.

3 Stir in the flour, cook for a few seconds, then mix in the stock. Return the chicken, stir in the herbs, season and bring to the boil. Cook uncovered for 10 minutes on a medium simmer, then pour into a shallow ovenproof dish. Meanwhile, preheat the oven to Gas Mark 5/190°C/375°F.

4 Arrange the thinly sliced potato on top. Brush quickly and lightly with the oil using a pastry brush (the oil will be easier to spread if you heat it first which you can do quickly in a cup in the microwave).

5 Bake uncovered for about 30 minutes until the top is golden brown and cooked.

Serves 3
Points per serving 7½
Total Points 23
Calories per serving 345

Turkey Pot Roast

800 g (1 lb 12 oz) turkey drumstick
1 tablespoon sunflower or olive oil
1 large onion, sliced
2 celery sticks, sliced thickly
2 carrots, sliced thickly
1 fat garlic clove, crushed
3 tomatoes, quartered
1 bay leaf
½ teaspoon dried mixed herbs
300 ml (10 fl oz) stock
salt and freshly ground black pepper

Freezing recommended • Preparation time: 15 minutes + 45 minutes – 1 hour cooking.

1 Preheat the oven to Gas Mark 4/180°C/350°F. Preheat a large non-stick frying-pan and when quite hot, brown the turkey drumstick on all sides, without any oil. If any fat runs drain it off. Place the drumstick in an ovenproof dish with a well-fitting lid.

2 Add the oil to the frying-pan and sauté the onion, celery, carrots and garlic for 5 minutes. Spoon into the dish with the turkey along with the tomatoes, bay leaf, herbs, stock and seasoning. Cover and bake for about 45–50 minutes until the drumstick is tender, basting it with the stock once or twice during cooking.

3 Check it is cooked by piercing the thickest part. If pink juices run out or the meat does not feel tender, then return it to bake for another 10–15 minutes.

Serves 4
Points per serving 6
Total Points 23½
Calories per serving 690

Spatchcock Grilled Chicken

2 x 1 kg (2 lb 4 oz) roasting chickens
1 tablespoon sunflower or olive oil
2 teaspoons ground paprika
2 teaspoons ground coriander
1 teaspoon dried mixed herbs
1 large lemon, cut into quarters, to serve
salt and freshly ground black pepper

Freezing not recommended • Preparation time: 10 minutes + 20 minutes marinating + 30 minutes cooking.

1 Remove any pads of fat from the birds and trim the bony ends of the legs. Cut off the neck flap and trim the 'parson's nose'. Turn the birds over and, using kitchen scissors and perhaps a sharp knife, cut the birds in half on the back bone side (not the breast bone side).

2 Mix the oil with the paprika, coriander and herbs. Pop the chicken and the spicy oil mixture into a polythene food bag and rub everything together. Leave in the fridge to marinate for about 20 minutes.

3 Meanwhile, preheat the grill to hot. Stick two long skewers diagonally through the birds to hold them open (known as spatchcocking).

4 Cook the chicken flesh-side up briefly under the hot grill to brown and then turn the heat down to medium. Cook on medium heat for about 20 minutes and then turn the birds over and cook for about 10 minutes on the underside.

5 Check if the chickens are cooked by piercing the flesh between the thigh and the breast. If pink juices run out and the flesh is still pink, then flip the chicken over and cook for longer on the fleshy side.

6 Season after cooking and then serve with the lemon quarters, which can be squeezed over the chicken at the table.

Orange and Tarragon Roast Chicken

1.25 kg (2 lb 12 oz) small roasting
    chicken
1 small orange, halved
2 teaspoon dried tarragon
300 g (10½ oz) large potato, peeled and
    sliced thickly
1 red onion, cut into thick slices (or an
    ordinary one)
1 large parsnip, peeled and cut into thick
    slices
2 tablespoons light soy sauce
2 tablespoons dry sherry (optional)
150 ml (5 fl oz) stock (optional)
2 tablespoons half-fat crème fraîche
salt and freshly ground black pepper

Freezing recommended if fresh chicken is used • Preparation and cooking time: 10 minutes + 1 hour cooking. Cooking meat and potatoes all in one is easy and satisfying – it also makes everything taste extra good.

1 Preheat the oven to Gas Mark 4/180°C/350°F. Cut as much fat off the bird as you can – the 'parson's nose', the pad of fat inside the body cavity and the neck flap. Squeeze the juice from the orange halves and set the juice aside. Put the orange halves inside the body cavity of the chicken.

2 Season the skin of the bird, sprinkle over the tarragon and cover the breast with a little foil. Place in the oven and start to cook for about 20 minutes.

3 Meanwhile, par-boil the potato and onion slices for 5 minutes and then drain. Mix the potatoes with the parsnip slices, soy sauce, sherry, if using, and then place around the bird in the chicken pan.

4 Return the chicken to the oven for another 30 minutes, turning the vegetables once or twice. Uncover the breast after 20 minutes and stir the vegetables.

5 Check the bird is cooked by piercing between the breast and thigh. If pink juices run out, return the bird to the oven to cook for longer.

6 When the chicken is cooked, place on a warm serving plate and cut into pieces to serve. Spoon the vegetables into a saucepan and add the orange juice, stock and crème fraîche. Bring to the boil and then serve with the chicken.

Weight Watchers note: If the recipe is made without sherry, deduct a ½ Point per serving.

Menu Plan

Breakfast		Lunch		Dinner	
Small glass fruit juice	½ Point	Medium slice toast	1 Point	**Just-got-in Stir-fry**	
Medium bowl 30 g (1¼ oz) Choco		Spread with a canned sardine, topped		(1 serving) page 64	9 Points
Krispies or Cornflakes	1½ Points	with	1 Point	2-inch piece French stick	1½ Points
¼ pint skimmed milk	½ Point	Sliced tomato		1 teaspoon low-fat spread	½ Point
		Side salad	0 Points	Apple	½ Point
		Large slice pineapple	½ Point		

Throughout the day: ¼ pint skimmed milk *1½ Points*   **Treat:** Small tub 150 g (5½ oz) low-fat yogurt *2 Points*

Serves 4 · Points per serving 3 · Total Points 11 · Calories per serving 195

Dijon Turkey

500 g (1 lb 2 oz) diced turkey meat

2 teaspoons sunflower oil

1 onion, sliced

1 fat garlic clove, crushed

2 teaspoons Dijon or French mustard

2 teaspoons coarse-grain mustard

a good pinch of dried tarragon or thyme

300 ml (10 fl oz) stock

3 tablespoons half-fat crème fraîche

salt and freshly ground black pepper

Freezing not recommended • Preparation time: 15 minutes + 15 minutes cooking. This classic dish from Dijon is normally made with cream but here is a lighter version which is just as good with half-fat crème fraîche.

1 Heat a large non-stick frying-pan and when quite hot, add the turkey meat. Stir well until nicely browned.

2 Remove the turkey with a slotted spoon and add the oil. When the oil is hot, add the onion and garlic. Cook, stirring once or twice, for 5 minutes and then return the turkey to the pan.

3 Stir in the two mustards and the tarragon or thyme. Cook for a few seconds and then stir in the stock and seasoning.

4 Bring to the boil. Simmer gently for 15 minutes until slightly reduced and the meat is tender. Mix in the crème fraîche, return to a simmer and cook for 2 minutes.

Serves 4 · Points per serving 5 · Total Points 19½ · Calories per serving 585

Chicken Hot-pot

1.5 kg (3 lb 5 oz) roasting chicken

1 onion, cut into thick chunks

2 celery sticks, sliced thickly

2 turnips

2 carrots, cut into thick slices

250 g (9 oz) new potatoes, halved if large

6 stoned no-need-to-soak prunes (optional)

2 bay leaves

a small handful of parsley sprigs, chopped
  and stalks removed and crushed

2 chicken stock cubes

salt and freshly ground black pepper

Freezing recommended • Preparation time: 15 minutes + 1 hour cooking + cooling (optional). The prunes are optional but add a nice old-English touch to the dish. Add 15 Calories. The Points per serving remain the same.

1 Trim the chicken of any obvious pads of fat. Cut off the leg tips, the fatty neck flap and the 'parson's nose'.

2 Place the chicken in a large saucepan with the vegetables, prunes, if using, bay leaves and parsley stalks. Just cover with cold water.

3 Bring to the boil slowly and then crumble in the stock cubes and add seasoning to taste. Cover and simmer very gently for 1 hour or until the bird and vegetables are tender.

4 To cut down on fat, if you wish, remove the bird and vegetables and cool in another dish in the fridge. Cool the stock separately in the fridge and then scrape off any fat which solidifies on top.

5 Reserve some of the stock to use as a light gravy. (The rest of the stock can be used to make a wonderful home-made soup.)

6 To serve, cut the chicken into pieces and then reheat with the vegetables in a little of the stock. Sprinkle over the chopped parsley leaves.

Serves 4

Points per serving 10
Total Points 40½
Calories per serving 510

Moroccan Chicken with Steamed Couscous

4 chicken quarters, skinned and trimmed
   of visible fat
1 tablespoon sunflower or olive oil
1 onion, sliced thickly
1 red pepper, de-seeded and sliced
2 carrots, cut into thick sticks
250 g (9 oz) potato, cut into thick chunks
1 large celery stick, sliced thickly
1 teaspoon ground turmeric
½ teaspoon ground cinnamon
1 teaspoon ground cumin
2 teaspoons ground coriander
1 bay leaf
450 ml (16 fl oz) stock
a few strips of lemon zest
juice of 1 lemon
a handful of fresh parsley or coriander
   sprigs, chopped
250 g (9 oz) couscous
salt and freshly ground black pepper

Freezing recommended ● Preparation time: 20 minutes + 45 minutes cooking. This dish is typical of Moroccan cooking which is often spicy and aromatic without being too hot. However, if you feel like turning up the heat, you can stir a spice paste called harissa into the juices of this stew.

1 Season the chicken lightly. Heat the oil in a large heavy-based saucepan and brown the quarters quickly. Remove and stir in the chunky vegetables. Add 3 tablespoons of water and then cover the pan. Cook gently for 5 minutes until softened, shaking the pan occasionally.

2 Stir in all the spices except the bay leaf. Cook for a minute and then add the bay leaf. Stir in the stock and add the lemon zest.

3 Bring the stock to the boil, then season and cover. Simmer very gently for about 45 minutes until the meat is tender. Stir in the lemon juice.

4 Meanwhile, soak and steam the couscous according to the pack instructions. Serve the chicken and vegetables on a bed of couscous with the parsley or coriander sprinkled on top.

Moroccan Chicken with Steamed Couscous

Menu Plan

Breakfast		Lunch		Dinner	
Medium bowl 30 g (1¼ oz) Rice		Small can 200 g (7 oz) ravioli in		**Chicken, Leek and Potato Pie**	
Krispies or Ready Brek	*1½ Points*	tomato sauce	*2½ Points*	(1 serving) page 64	*7½ Points*
¼ pint skimmed milk	*½ Point*	4-inch slice French stick	*3 Points*	Carrots, broccoli	*0 Points*
		2 teaspoons low-fat spread	*1 Point*	1 tablespoon peas	*½ Point*
		Peach or nectarine	*½ Point*	2 satsumas or tangerines	*½ Point*

Throughout the day: ¾ pint skimmed milk *1½ Points*   **Treat:** Small glass wine *1 Point*

Points per serving 5

Total Points 21

Calories per serving 220

Turkey Burgers

500 g (1 lb 2 oz) turkey mince

1 small onion, grated or chopped very
 finely

2 tablespoons soy sauce

1 teaspoon garlic powder

½ teaspoon dried mixed herbs

low-fat cooking spray

2 medium wholemeal pitta breads

freshly ground black pepper

To serve:

iceberg or Little Gem lettuce, shredded
 finely

cucumber, sliced thinly

2 tablespoons low-fat plain yogurt

Freezing not recommended • Preparation time: 10 minutes + 15 minutes cooking. Minced turkey is very lean; in many cases it has less than 5% fat. And yet it holds together well so it is ideal for home-made burgers which your family will love.

1 Place the turkey mince, grated onion, soy sauce, garlic and herbs along with the freshly ground black pepper to taste, in a bowl. Mix together well.

2 Divide into four and using hands dipped in cold water, shape the mixture into flat even burgers. Press the meat firmly so that it holds together well.

3 Preheat a heavy-based non-stick frying-pan until quite hot and then cover with the cooking spray.

4 Over a medium heat, cook the burgers for about 5 to 7 minutes on each side or until they feel quite firm when pressed. Remove the pan from the heat but leave the burgers in the pan to keep them warm.

5 Meanwhile, warm the pitta breads for a few seconds either in a microwave or under a grill. Cut each pitta in half to make half moon shapes and open up carefully.

6 Toss the shredded lettuce with the cucumber and yogurt. Season to taste. Fill the pittas with the salad and burgers and eat immediately.

Serves 2

Points per serving 10

Total Points 19

Calories per serving 405

Chicken and Bacon Kebabs

2 x 250 g (9 oz) skinless, boneless
 chicken, each cut into 4 chunks

a few pinches of dried sage

4 rashers of lean streaky bacon, de-rinded

1 onion, peeled, quartered and separated
 into leaves

salt and freshly ground black pepper

Freezing not recommended • Preparation and cooking time: 25 minutes. Serve with a crisp salad of shredded lettuce, tomato and cucumber.

1 Sprinkle the chicken with tiny pinches of sage and season to taste.

2 Stretch the rashers with the back of a table knife by holding the rasher down and running the back of the knife down the length of the rasher to make it longer. Then cut each rasher in half.

3 Wrap each chicken chunk with bacon and then thread them on to a skewer, alternating with the onion 'leaves'.

4 Preheat the grill and when hot, place each kebab on the grill rack. Turn the heat down to medium.

5 Grill on medium heat for 5 minutes on each side or until the meat feels quite firm when pressed.

Turkey Burgers

Chicken and Bacon Kebabs

Serves **4**

Points per serving 5½
Total Points 21
Calories per serving 345

Chilli Roasted Turkey Strips

500 g (1 lb 2 oz) lean turkey steaks, cut
　　into 2 cm (¾-inch) strips
1 tablespoon sunflower oil
2 teaspoons mild chilli powder
1 teaspoon garlic granules
1 teaspoon ground cumin
2 teaspoons ground coriander
1 teaspoon dried oregano or marjoram
3 tablespoons very-low-fat fromage frais
salt and freshly ground black pepper
To serve:
4 medium pitta breads or soft medium
　　tortillas
shredded lettuce

**Freezing not recommended • Preparation time: 5 minutes + 20
minutes marinating + 30 minutes cooking.** Turkey steaks are now
quite easy to find in the supermarket chill cabinets. In this recipe, they
are roasted in a foil parcel which gathers together all the delicious
juices and helps to keep the meat moist.

1　Place the turkey strips in a bowl along with the oil, chilli powder,
garlic, cumin, coriander, oregano or marjoram. Add black pepper to taste.
2　Mix together well and then cover and chill for 20 minutes.
3　Meanwhile, preheat the oven to Gas Mark 5/190°C/375°F. Tip the
turkey strips on to a large sheet of foil and fold up loosely to form a
parcel, scrunching the edges together well to seal.
4　Place the parcel on a baking sheet and roast for 20 minutes, then
open up the parcel. Stir the turkey, season with salt and then return to
the oven to cook for another 10 minutes until lightly browned.
5　Serve on a large plate with the juices trickled over. Stir the fromage
frais until runny and then spoon on top of the turkey. Serve with
warmed pitta or try wrapping the turkey in soft, warmed tortillas, with
the shredded lettuce.

Variation: If you use tortillas, deduct a ½ Point per serving.

Serves **2**

Points per serving 10½
Total Points 21½
Calories per serving 810

Chicken Chow Mein

2 medium skinless, boneless chicken
　　breasts, cut into bite-size chunks
3 tablespoons light soy sauce
1 tablespoon dry sherry
2 teaspoons cornflour
2 x 125 g (4½ oz) 'nests' of Chinese egg
　　noodles
1 teaspoon sesame seed oil
1 tablespoon sunflower oil
1 large pack of ready-prepared stir-fry
　　vegetables

**Freezing not recommended • Preparation and cooking time: 25
minutes.** Chow mein is perhaps the best known Chinese dish outside
China! It is an all-in-one meal and very easy to prepare. Save yourself
some time by buying a pack of prepared stir-fry mixed vegetables.

1　Mix the chunks of chicken with 1 tablespoon of soy sauce, sherry
and cornflour. Set aside for about 5 minutes.
2　Soak the noodles in boiling water according to the pack instructions.
Drain and toss with the sesame oil.
3　Heat the sunflower oil in a large non-stick wok and stir-fry the
chicken quickly, tossing it well to separate.
4　Mix in the vegetables and stir-fry for 2 to 3 minutes, then add the
remaining soy sauce. Toss everything with the noodles and serve
immediately in two bowls. Serve with chop sticks – it's good fun!

Meat

6

Lean meat is very nutritious and because it has lots of
protein and is a rich source of iron, zinc and B vitamins, it is
an important part of a healthy diet. The ready-trimmed cuts
of meat are excellent when you are trying to lose
weight and they are so easy to use. When you get
it home, if there is any visible fat, make sure
that you trim it off before cooking.
Meat is very versatile; there are so many
different types and cuts of meat which can be
cooked in any number of ways. Whether you feel
like some quick Lamb Chops with a Fruity Glaze or
an Old-Fashioned Lamb Hot Pot to treat family and friends,
you'll find lots of delicious and healthy recipes to choose
from in this chapter.

Simple Beef Stew with Dumplings

low-fat cooking spray

500 g (1 lb 2 oz) lean topside, top rump or silverside of beef, trimmed of all fat and cubed

1 onion, sliced

1 teaspoon garlic purée

2 carrots, cut into thick sticks

1 celery stick, sliced

450 ml (16 fl oz) beef stock

1 tablespoon Worcestershire sauce

1 bay leaf

2 tablespoons cornflour

1 tablespoon chopped fresh parsley (optional)

salt and freshly ground black pepper

For the dumplings:

50 g (1$\frac{3}{4}$ oz) self-raising flour

$\frac{1}{2}$ teaspoon baking powder

$\frac{1}{2}$ teaspoon salt

3 teaspoons sunflower or soya margarine (not reduced-fat margarine)

50 g (1$\frac{3}{4}$ oz) fresh breadcrumbs

$\frac{1}{4}$ teaspoon dried thyme

Freezing recommended • Preparation time: 20 minutes + 1$\frac{1}{4}$ hours cooking. Comfort food at its best.

1 Heat a large non-stick saucepan and when quite hot, spray with the cooking spray and add the meat. Stir-fry quickly to brown and then remove.

2 Add the onion, garlic, carrots and celery to the pan with 4 table-spoons of the stock. Bring to the boil, then cover and cook very gently for 5 minutes, until softened. Add the remaining stock, the Worcestershire sauce and the bay leaf. Return the meat to the pan.

3 Season, then bring to the boil and cover. Turn the heat right down to bring the stew to a gentle simmer and cook for about 50 minutes, until the meat is tender.

4 Meanwhile, make up the dumpling mixture. Sift the flour with the baking powder and salt and then rub in the margarine until it resembles coarse breadcrumbs. Mix in the breadcrumbs and thyme. Set aside.

5 When the meat is tender, blend the cornflour with 2 tablespoons of cold water, add to the stew and stir briskly until the stew is thickened.

6 To finish the dumplings, add 2 to 3 tablespoons of cold water to the dry mix and stir together quickly until you have a firm but not sticky dough. Divide the dough into 4 balls and drop on to the simmering stew.

7 Cover and continue cooking (on a gentle heat or else you will break up the dumplings) for another 20 minutes or so. To serve, sprinkle the stew and dumplings with a little chopped parsley for a nice homely touch.

Cooks' notes: A lean, slow-roasting cut such as topside or top rump will not take as long to cook until tender.

To make fresh breadcrumbs, simply grate a small slice of 2-day-old bread or pop it in to a food processor.

Weight Watchers note: If using top rump, the Points per serving will be 4; if using silverside, the Points per serving will be 4$\frac{1}{2}$.

Simple Beef Stew with Dumplings
Steak with Herb Butter *(page 77)*

Serves **4**

Points per serving 5
Total Points 19
Calories per serving 260

low-fat cooking spray
500 g (1 lb 2 oz) extra-lean beef mince
3 tablespoons white wine or 2 tablespoons
  dry sherry (optional)
400 g (14 oz) canned chopped tomatoes
  with garlic
2 tablespoons tomato purée
1 tablespoon soy sauce or Worcestershire
  sauce
½ teaspoon dried oregano or marjoram
3 tablespoons half-fat crème fraîche
salt and freshly ground black pepper

Quick Beef and Tomato Pasta Sauce

Freezing recommended • Preparation time: 10 minutes + 10 minutes cooking. Buy good quality steak mince for this recipe; not only is it leaner, it also cooks more quickly.

1 Heat a large non-stick frying-pan and when hot, spray with the low-fat cooking spray. Add the mince and stir to break up any lumps as it browns. Make sure it is nice and crumbly.

2 Add the wine or sherry, if using, and cook until reduced by half and then pour in the chopped tomatoes. Bring to the boil, stirring, and mix in the tomato purée, the soy or Worcestershire sauce, herbs and seasoning.

3 Simmer, uncovered for about 10 minutes until thickened and then stir in the crème fraîche just before serving.

Weight Watcher's note: The Points will remain the same if you decide to add wine or sherry.

Serves **4**

Points per serving 7
Total Points 27½
Calories per serving 630

1 large red onion, sliced thickly (or an
  ordinary one)
2 celery sticks, sliced thickly
1 large parsnip, cut into thick slices
2 large carrots, cut into thick sticks
1 large green pepper, de-seeded and sliced
  thickly
1 tablespoon sunflower oil
½ teaspoon dried mixed herbs
700 g (1 lb 9 oz) lean joint of beef topside,
  trimmed of all fat
450 ml (16 fl oz) beef stock (plus some
  extra if required)
1 tablespoon tomato purée or soy sauce
2 tablespoons cornflour
salt and freshly ground black pepper

Slow-cook Beef Roast

Freezing recommended • Preparation time: 15 minutes + 1¼–1½ hours cooking. Brown a lean piece of topside in a hot oven on a bed of vegetables, then cover and cook slowly at a lower temperature.

1 Preheat the oven to Gas Mark 7/220°C/425°F.

2 Place all the vegetables in a polythene food bag with the oil, herbs and seasoning. Shake well to mix.

3 Tip into a small roasting pan and place the joint on top.

4 Roast for 15 minutes until the meat is sealed and the vegetables lightly browned. Reduce the heat to Gas Mark 3/170°C/325°F.

5 Meanwhile, bring the stock to the boil and stir in the purée or soy sauce, then pour this around the vegetables. Cover the meat and vegetables lightly with a sheet of foil but leave some of the foil untucked to allow the steam to escape.

6 Roast until the meat is tender and the vegetables are softened (about 1 hour). When the meat is cooked, remove it and keep warm. If the stock has evaporated, add extra to replace it and then place the pan, with the vegetables still inside, on the hob on a medium heat.

7 Blend the cornflour with 2 tablespoons of water, add to the pan, and stir briskly until the liquid thickens. Cut the meat into thin slices and serve with the vegetables and 'gravy'.

Points per serving 4

Serves 4 Total Points 15½

Calories per serving 285

500 g (1 lb 2 oz) lean braising beef

2 tablespoons flour

½ teaspoon dried mixed herbs

1 onion, sliced thinly

500 g (1 lb 2 oz) ready-prepared
vegetables e.g. carrots, swede, celery

150 ml (5 fl oz) dry cider or flat lager

400 ml (14 fl oz) beef stock

1 tablespoon wine vinegar

1 tablespoon tomato purée

1 teaspoon sugar

1 large bay leaf

salt and freshly ground black pepper

Beef and Cider Casserole

Freezing recommended • Preparation time: 15 minutes + 1¼ hours cooking. This recipe is so easy; just mix together the ingredients and then leave to cook.

1 Preheat the oven to Gas Mark 4/180°C/350°F. Cover the meat with the flour, herbs, black pepper and 1 teaspoon of salt.

2 Place the meat in a cast iron casserole. Add the onion, vegetables, cider or lager, stock, vinegar, tomato purée, sugar and bay leaf.

3 Bring to the boil, stirring well until everything is mixed together well and then cover tightly. Cook in the oven for 1 hour.

4 Stir the contents once or twice during cooking if possible, but this is not absolutely necessary. The meat should be cooked within an hour, depending on the quality of the meat. If not, then continue cooking for another 15 minutes or so.

Points per serving 3

Serves 4 Total Points 13

Calories per serving 170

3 tablespoons very-low-fat spread

2 garlic cloves, crushed, or 2 teaspoons
garlic purée

2 tablespoons chopped fresh parsley

grated zest of ½ lemon

a good pinch of dried thyme or mixed herbs

low-fat cooking spray

4 x 100 g (3½ oz) frying beef steaks e.g.
sirloin or rump

salt and freshly ground black pepper

Steak with Herb Butter

Freezing: only recommended for the butter • Preparation time: 10 minutes + 1 hour chilling + 10 minutes cooking. Keep these 'steak butters' in the freezer ready to pop on top of a grilled or dry-fried steak. This works nicely with chops too. If you wish, you could easily double or treble this recipe and freeze some for later.

1 Put the low-fat spread into a bowl and mix in the garlic, parsley, lemon zest, ¼ teaspoon pepper and dried herbs. Beat together well and then spoon on to a sheet of foil.

2 Roll the mixture into sausage shape and chill for an hour until solid. Then cut into four pats using a serrated knife.

3 To cook the steaks, preheat a heavy-based non-stick frying-pan and spray with the cooking spray. When the pan feels quite hot, season the steaks lightly and cook for 3–5 minutes on each side, depending on how you like them. Medium-rare steaks will feel quite springy; well-done steaks will be quite firm.

4 Remove to warm serving plates and top each steak with a pat of herb butter.

Weight Watcher's note: The rump steak will reduce the Points by a ½ Point per serving.

Quick Balti Beef

250 g (9 oz) lean minced beef

1 small onion, chopped finely

2 garlic cloves, crushed or 2 teaspoons
garlic purée

1 teaspoon ginger purée

1 teaspoon green chilli purée (optional)

1–2 teaspoons mild curry powder, to
taste

300 ml (10 fl oz) stock (any sort) or water

1 tablespoon chutney

1 tablespoon chopped fresh coriander or
parsley (optional)

2 tablespoons low-fat plain yogurt

salt and freshly ground black pepper

Freezing recommended • **Preparation time: 5 minutes + 15 minutes cooking.** Balti cooking is rather like stir-frying a curry! Serve with plain basmati rice or naan bread.

1 Heat a large non-stick wok and when hot, dry-fry the mince, stirring continuously, until crumbly and browned.

2 Add the onion, garlic, ginger and chilli, if using, along with the curry powder. Stir well and cook for 2 minutes.

3 Stir in the stock, chutney and seasoning. Bring to the boil and then turn down the heat and simmer for 5 minutes until reduced and the mince is cooked.

4 Sprinkle over the coriander, if using, and serve hot, topped with yogurt.

Variation: Replace the beef with turkey and deduct a ¹/₂ Point per serving.

Easy Shepherd's Pie *(page 81)*
Quick Balti Beef

Serves 4
Points per serving 6
Total Points 24½
Calories per serving 355

Stuffed Marrow

1.5 kg (3 lb 5 oz) marrow, cut in half
    lengthways and de-seeded
500 g (1 lb 2 oz) extra lean beef mince
1 tablespoon sunflower oil
1 onion, chopped
2 carrots, grated coarsely
400 g (14 oz) canned chopped tomatoes
300 ml (10 fl oz) beef or chicken stock
½ teaspoon dried mixed herbs
100 g (3½ oz) fresh breadcrumbs
15 g (½ oz) grated fresh parmesan cheese
salt and freshly ground black pepper

Freezing recommended • Preparation time: 10 minutes + 40 minutes cooking. Protected by a tough outer skin, marrows last for quite a long time. They are also cheap and tasty with a variety of fillings. Serve these stuffed marrows with a green vegetable.

1 Using a sharp spoon and a small knife, scoop out as much of the flesh as possible from the marrow. Discard the seeds and chop the flesh.

2 Boil the marrow shells in a large saucepan for about 10 minutes, just to soften, and then drain them upside down.

3 Heat a large non-stick frying-pan and when hot, dry-fry the mince, stirring frequently to make sure there are no lumps. Remove the mince and add the oil to the pan.

4 Stir-fry the onion, chopped marrow and carrots for about 5 minutes until softened. Return the mince to the pan and then mix in the tomatoes, stock, herbs and seasoning.

5 Bring to the boil, then simmer uncovered for about 10 minutes until the liquid has been reduced and the meat and vegetables are cooked. Stir in three-quarters of the breadcrumbs and preheat the grill to a medium heat.

6 Lay the marrow shells in a shallow heatproof dish and spoon in the filling. Mix the parmesan cheese with the rest of the breadcrumbs and sprinkle over the filling.

7 Place the stuffed marrows under the grill and brown the topping until golden brown.

Variation: Replace the beef with turkey mince and deduct a ½ Point per serving.

Menu Plan

Breakfast		Lunch		Dinner	
Small glass fruit juice	½ Point	2 medium slices bread	2 Points	Beef and Cider Casserole	
Boiled egg	1½ Points	Medium portion 60 g (2¼ oz) prawns		(1 serving) page 77	4 Points
Medium slice bread	1 Point	mixed with	1 Point	3 scoops mashed potato	3 Points
1 teaspoon low-fat spread	½ Point	1 tablespoon low-fat mayonnaise		Pear sliced into	1 Point
			1 Point	Small tub low-fat plain yogurt	
		Shredded lettuce	0 Points		1½ Points
		Kiwi fruit	1 Point		

Throughout the day: ½ pint skimmed milk *1 Point*   **Treat:** Small bunch 100 g (3½ oz) grapes *1 Point*

Serves 4

Points per serving 9½

Total Points 37

Calories per serving 420

700 g (1 lb 9 oz) floury potatoes, peeled and cut into even chunks

2 teaspoons low-fat spread

4 tablespoons skimmed milk

a little freshly grated nutmeg

500 g (1 lb 2 oz) lean minced beef

2 teaspoons sunflower oil

1 onion, chopped finely

2 teaspoons garlic purée

1 carrot, peeled and grated coarsely

275 g (9½ oz) canned condensed beef consommé

a good pinch of dried mixed herbs

2 tablespoons natural colour breadcrumbs

1 tablespoon grated fresh parmesan cheese

salt and freshly ground black pepper

Easy Shepherd's Pie

Freezing recommended • Preparation time: 15 minutes + 30 minutes cooking. Always a favourite with the family, this is delicious with peas or broccoli on the side.

1 Boil the potatoes until just tender, then drain well and return to the pan. Heat until dry and floury, then mash the potatoes until smooth and lump free.

2 Mix in the low-fat spread, milk, nutmeg and seasoning. Set aside.

3 Dry-fry the mince in a very hot preheated non-stick frying-pan, stirring well to break up any lumps.

4 Add the oil and then the onion, garlic and carrot. Cook for 5 minutes until the vegetables soften, then stir in the consommé and 150 ml (5 fl oz) of water plus the herbs and seasoning.

5 Simmer uncovered for 10 minutes until the meat is cooked and the liquid has been reduced. Stir once or twice during cooking.

6 Preheat the grill to a medium heat. Spoon the meat into a heatproof pie dish and spread the mashed potato roughly on top, with a fork. Sprinkle over the crumbs and cheese.

7 Place the pie dish under the grill and brown the top of the pie.

Variations: Replace the beef with turkey and deduct 2 Points per serving. Replace the beef with pork and deduct 1½ Points per serving.

Serves 4

Points per serving 7½

Total points 29

Calories per serving 375

500 g (1 lb 2 oz) lean lamb mince

1 onion, chopped finely

1 celery stick, chopped

1 carrot, grated coarsely

2 tomatoes, chopped

2 tablespoons brown sauce

450 ml (16 fl oz) stock or water

½ teaspoon dried mixed herbs

500 g (1 lb 2 oz) large potatoes, peeled and sliced very thinly

1 teaspoon sunflower oil

salt and freshly ground black pepper

Old-fashioned Lamb Hot-Pot

Freezing recommended • Preparation time: 25 minutes + 25 minutes cooking. This is a good dish to make ahead and freeze for later.

1 Preheat the oven to Gas Mark 5/190°C/375°F. Preheat a non-stick frying-pan and when quite hot, dry-fry the mince, stirring frequently, to break up the lumps so the meat is crumbly. Drain off the fat.

2 Add the onion, celery and carrot to the pan, stirring well, and cook for about 5 minutes until softened.

3 Stir in the tomatoes, brown sauce, stock, herbs and seasoning. Bring to the boil and then simmer for about 10 minutes.

4 When the mince is cooked, tip everything into a shallow ovenproof dish and arrange the potatoes on top in a single layer. Using a pastry brush, brush the top lightly with the oil.

5 Bake for about 25 minutes until the top is golden brown and cooked.

Points per serving 5
Total Points 19½
Calories per serving 290

Chinese Chicken Liver Stir-fry

225 g (8 oz) chicken livers, thawed if frozen
2 medium skinless, boneless chicken breasts, cut into small cubes
3 tablespoons soy sauce
2 teaspoons cornflour
1 tablespoon sunflower oil
1 onion, sliced thinly
1 pack of ready-prepared stir-fry vegetables of your choice
½ teaspoon Chinese five-spice powder (optional)
125 g (4½ oz) button mushrooms (optional)
2 tablespoons dry sherry
1 teaspoon clear honey
1 teaspoon sesame seed oil
1 teaspoon sesame seeds or 2 tablespoons chopped fresh coriander
salt and freshly ground black pepper

Freezing not recommended • Preparation time: 25 minutes.
Chicken livers are not only nutritious, they are also cheap and tasty. If you need to thaw out the livers in a hurry, put them in the microwave for 12–15 minutes on the defrost setting. Serve with rice or hot egg noodles.

1 Using kitchen scissors, trim the livers into neat shapes. Mix the liver and the chicken with 1 tablespoon of soy sauce and the cornflour. Leave for 5 minutes.
2 Heat half the oil in a non-stick wok and quickly stir-fry the meats for about 2 minutes until just firm. Remove to a dish.
3 Heat the remaining oil in the wok and stir-fry the onion with the prepared vegetables. Add the five-spice powder, if using. Cook for about 2 minutes, then add the mushrooms and return the meat and cook for another 2 minutes.
4 Stir in the remaining soy sauce, sherry, honey and sesame oil. Heat through. Season to taste and then serve sprinkled with sesame seeds or coriander.

Points per serving 4½
Total Points 9½
Calories per serving 170

Devilled Lamb's Kidneys

4 lamb's kidneys
2 teaspoons sunflower or olive oil
1 red onion, sliced thinly (or an ordinary one)
1 fat garlic clove, crushed
a pinch of dried thyme
1 tablespoon French or coarse-grain mustard
2 teaspoons Worcestershire sauce
2 tablespoons very low-fat fromage frais
1 tablespoon chopped fresh parsley
salt and freshly ground black pepper

Freezing recommended • Preparation and cooking time: 20 minutes. Kidneys are very high in protein yet they are low in fat, so they are ideal if you are watching your weight. They are also good sources of minerals and vitamins, particularly iron. Don't overcook them though or they become tough.

1 First, prepare the kidneys. Cut them in half lengthways and then, using kitchen scissors, cut out the core. Peel off any membrane (the butcher may have done this already) and then cut each half into quarters.
2 Heat the oil in a non-stick frying-pan and when hot quickly stir-fry the kidneys until sealed, then stir in the onion, garlic and thyme.
3 Cook on a medium heat for about 5 minutes, then stir in the mustard, Worcestershire sauce and 3–4 tablespoons of water. Season and simmer for a minute or two, then remove from the heat and mix in the fromage frais and parsley.

Chinese Chicken Liver Stir-fry
Devilled Lamb's Kidneys

Serves 4 | Points per serving 4½
Total Points 17½
Calories per serving 295

French Lamb Stew

500 g (1 lb 2 oz) very lean leg of lamb,
trimmed of all fat and cubed

1 tablespoon sunflower or olive oil

2 small onions, quartered

2 celery sticks, sliced thickly

4 baby carrots, trimmed and halved

2 small turnips, peeled and halved

2 tablespoons flour

450 ml (16 fl oz) beef or lamb stock

1 bay leaf

¼ teaspoon dried thyme

2 tablespoons tomato purée

1 teaspoon sugar

125 g (4½ oz) frozen broad beans

salt and freshly ground black pepper

Freezing recommended • Preparation time: 20 minutes + 20 minutes cooking. This traditional French stew is normally a slow-cooked dish of lamb and root vegetables. However, today's quick-cook cuts of lamb and tender young vegetables make it possible to enjoy an authentic-tasting stew in no time at all.

1 Heat a large, heavy-based non-stick saucepan and when hot, stir-fry the lamb with half the oil until just browned. Remove with a slotted spoon.

2 Add the remaining oil to the pan and sauté all the vegetables gently for 5 minutes. Sprinkle over the flour, stir in and cook for 1 minute.

3 Pour in the stock, stirring, and bring to the boil. Then mix in the bay leaf, thyme, tomato purée, sugar, broad beans and seasoning.

4 Return the meat to the pan and simmer gently, uncovered, for about 20 minutes or until the meat is tender.

French Lamb Stew

Menu Plan

Breakfast		Lunch		Dinner	
Small glass fruit juice	½ Point	2 slices 35 g (1¼) each honey roast		**French Lamb Stew**	
2 medium slices toast	2 Points	ham	2 Points	(1 serving), above	4½ Points
2 teaspoons low-fat spread	1 Point	2 tablespoons potato salad	2 Points	Medium portion 200 g (7 oz) boiled	
2 heaped teaspoons jam or marmalade		Lettuce, tomato, spring onions,		potatoes	2 Points
	1 Point	beetroot	0 Points	Green beans, cauliflower	0 Points
		Orange	½ Point	Small can 210 g (7½ oz) fruit cocktail	
				in juice	1 Point
				Small tub low-fat plain yogurt	
					1½ Points

Throughout the day: ½ pint skimmed milk *1 Point* **Treat:** Small glass wine *1 Point*

Serves 2

Points per serving 6½

Total Points 13½

Calories per serving 180

2 x 150 g (5½ oz) loin of lamb chops, trimmed of all fat

2 pinches of dried thyme or crushed rosemary

2 teaspoons coarse-grain mustard

2 teaspoons redcurrant jelly

1 teaspoon lemon juice

salt and freshly ground black pepper

Lamb Chops with a Fruity Glaze

Freezing not recommended • Preparation time: 10 minutes + 10–15 minutes grilling. A mustard and redcurrant glaze makes these chops taste truly wonderful. Serve with some mashed potato and some lightly boiled Savoy cabbage.

1 Preheat the grill until piping hot. Sprinkle the chops with half the herbs and season with pepper only.

2 Put the chops on the grill rack and turn the heat down to medium. Grill for about 5–7 minutes on each side depending on whether you like lamb medium or well-done.

3 Meanwhile, mix the mustard, redcurrant jelly and lemon juice together. About 4 minutes from the end of cooking on the second side, spoon the glaze on both chops.

4 Return to the grill to finish cooking. When the chops are cooked, season with salt and pepper.

Serves 4

Points per serving 4

Total Points 16½

Calories per serving 185

4 x 100 g (3½ oz) uncooked ham or gammon steaks, trimmed of all fat

low-fat cooking spray

200 g (7 oz) canned apricot halves in natural juice, drained and chopped roughly, reserving 2 tablespoons juice

1 tablespoon white wine vinegar

1 tablespoon light soft brown sugar

a good pinch of ground cinnamon

1 pickled onion, sliced

freshly ground black pepper

Ham Steaks with Sweet and Sour Apricots

Freezing not recommended • Preparation time: 5 minutes + 15 minutes cooking. Ham or gammon steaks are now sold very lean with a thin layer of fat on top which can easily be removed. A quick relish with apricots is the perfect accompaniment.

1 Make small cuts into the edges of the steaks so that they will stay flat during cooking.

2 Heat a large non-stick frying-pan and spray with low-fat cooking spray. Add the steaks and cook for 5 minutes on each side. Remove and keep warm.

3 Put the chopped apricots, vinegar, sugar, cinnamon and onion into the pan along with the two reserved spoons of juice. Season with pepper. Bring to a boil and simmer for about 3 minutes, stirring occasionally. Spoon on to the warmed ham steaks and serve hot.

Lamb Chops with a Fruity Glaze
Ham Steaks with Sweet and Sour Apricots

Points per serving 5
Total Points 19½
Calories per serving 305

Honey-mustard Roast Pork

1–1.25 kg (2 lb 4 oz–2 lb 12 oz) rolled
    boned leg of pork
3 garlic cloves, slivered
1 large sprig of rosemary, separated into
    small tips
1 tablespoon coarse-grain mustard
1 tablespoon clear honey
salt and freshly ground black pepper

Freezing recommended if fresh pork is used • Preparation time: 15 minutes + 1 hour cooking. Serve with baked potatoes filled with garlic-flavoured low-fat soft cheese and a green salad.

1 Untie the joint and remove all the fat and any rind. With a sharp knife, stab the joint several times on the top. Re-tie the joint with clean kitchen string, if you wish.

2 Stick a garlic sliver and rosemary tip into each hole made by the knife and season lightly.

3 Let the joint stand while you preheat the oven to Gas Mark 4/180°C/350°F. Place the joint in a small roasting-pan and cover the top with a small sheet of foil so it is still open around the sides. Roast for about an hour, periodically brushing over any roasting juices.

4 Mix the mustard and honey and twenty minutes before the end of cooking, uncover and brush the mustard and honey all over the pork with a pastry brush. The meat should take on a glossy glaze. You may have to brush over any glaze which has slipped into the pan a few minutes before the end of cooking.

5 Check the meat is cooked by piercing it with a thin metal skewer. Only clear juice should run out. If the juice is a bit pink, then cook for a little longer.

Weight Watcher's note: Points and Calories are based on 150 g (5½ oz) servings of pork.

Vegetarian
Meals

Chapter

7

Vegetarian meals are something everyone can enjoy. They are cheap and offer a refreshing and healthy alternative to fish and meat. Thanks to the ever-widening selection of vegetables in the supermarkets, we can now explore lots of different tastes all year round.

Vegetarian meals can be very convenient, especially once you realise how many canned, packet and frozen foods are ideal to use; just throw together some store cupboard and packet ingredients and a vegetarian dinner will be on the table in no time at all. Vegetarian cooking is typically very flavoursome since many vegetarian dishes come from places like India where plenty of herbs and spices are used. And that's ideal when you are on a diet: lots of taste without lots of Points and Calories.

Serves 4

Points per serving 2
Total Points 8
Calories per serving 95

250 g (9 oz) open-cup mushrooms, sliced
thinly

2 salad onions, chopped finely

1 tablespoon soy sauce

2 tablespoons low-fat fromage frais

1 tablespoon chopped fresh parsley
(optional)

4 x 30 cm (12-inch) square sheets of filo
pastry

4 teaspoons low-fat spread, melted

salt and freshly ground black pepper

Mushroom Pasties

Ⓥ **Freezing not recommended • Preparation and cooking time: 40
minutes.** Filo pastry is so easy to use and is great for dieters since a
little goes a long way.

1 Put the mushrooms, salad onions and soy sauce into a saucepan,
with 5 tablespoons of water and some seasoning. Bring to a sizzle, then
cover the pan, lower the heat and cook for about 5 minutes until the
mushrooms have softened. Drain and cool, then mix in the fromage
frais and parsley. Set aside.

2 Preheat the oven to Gas Mark 5/190°C/375°F. Take a sheet of filo
pastry and brush quickly with a quarter of the melted low-fat spread.
Fold in half lengthways.

3 Put a quarter of the cool filling at the top, fold in the sides down the
full length of pastry and then roll up to make a pasty. Repeat with the
remaining 3 filo sheets so that you have a total of four pasties.

4 Place the pasties joint-side down on a flat baking sheet. If you have
any melted low-fat spread left over, brush this lightly on top. Bake for
20 minutes until crisp and golden brown. Remove to a wire tray to
cool slightly. Eat warm.

Serves 4

Points per serving 5½
Total Points 22
Calories per serving 325

150 g (5½ oz) self-raising flour

½ teaspoon baking powder

1 teaspoon dried mixed herbs

40 g (1½ oz) sunflower margarine (not
low-fat)

4 tablespoons skimmed milk, plus extra for
glazing

400 g (14 oz) canned Weight Watchers
from Heinz baked beans

200 g (7 oz) canned sweetcorn

1 tablespoon chilli relish or brown sauce or
soy sauce

salt and freshly ground black pepper

Baked Bean Cobbler

Ⓥ **Freezing not recommended • Preparation time: 25 minutes + 20
minutes cooking.** This is easy, filling and healthy.

1 Preheat the oven to Gas Mark 5/190°C/375°F. Sift the flour,
½ teaspoon salt and baking powder together. Then mix in the herbs.
Using your fingertips, rub in the margarine until the mixture resembles
fine crumbs.

2 Add ¾ of the milk and make a firm dough adding more milk as
necessary. You may need some more milk, but don't allow the dough to
get sticky. Divide the dough into four balls, patting them gently into
round shapes about 1 cm (½-inch) thick.

3 Tip the beans into a medium-size shallow ovenproof dish. Drain the
sweetcorn and mix in along with the sauce. Season and stir.

4 Drop the scones on top, brush with a little extra milk. Bake for
about 20 minutes until the scones are risen and golden.

Braised Celery Hearts with Butter Beans *(page 95)*
Mushroom Pasties

Serves 4
Points per serving ½
Total Points 2
Calories per serving 60

1 large cucumber

2 salad onions

1 tablespoon fresh chopped dill or 1
teaspoon dried dill weed

200 g (7 oz) carton of skimmed milk soft
cheese, such as quark

1 sachet of vegetarian setting gel

a few sprigs of fresh dill, to garnish
(optional)

salt and freshly ground black pepper

Cucumber Mousse

 Freezing not recommended • Preparation time: 15 minutes +
draining + setting. When the sun is shining, this cool, savoury mousse
is very refreshing. It can be served as a light summer meal or as a first
course for a special supper. Let it set in a pretty bowl and scoop it out
right at the table. Rye crispbread is ideal with it.

1 Cut about 4 thin slices of the cucumber to be used later as a garnish.
Set aside. Halve the rest of the cucumber lengthways and scoop out the
seeds. Chop the flesh roughly and then place in a colander, sprinkle
over one teaspoon of salt and mix in.

2 Leave for 20 minutes. This helps to make the cucumber less watery.
Pat dry with kitchen paper – there is no need to rinse.

3 Place the cucumber in a food processor with the salad onions, dill
and black pepper. Whizz to a purée and then add the skimmed milk
soft cheese. Blend until smooth and creamy.

4 Dissolve the setting gel according to the pack instructions and fold
in. Pour into a small bowl and chill until set. Garnish with the reserved
cucumber and any frilly fronds of dill, if using.

Serves 2
Points per serving 4
Total Points 8
Calories per serving 245

3 large free-range eggs

2 teaspoons olive oil (ideally extra-virgin
for flavour) or sunflower oil

1 onion, sliced thinly

1 small green pepper, de-seeded and sliced

1 small red pepper, de-seeded and sliced

1 fat garlic clove, crushed or 1 teaspoon
garlic purée

1 large firm tomato, chopped

1 tablespoon chopped fresh basil or 4
teaspoon dried

salt and freshly ground black pepper

Pipérade (Egg, Sweet Pepper and Tomato Bake)

 Freezing not recommended • Preparation and cooking time: 20
minutes. Eggs form the basis of many quick, satisfying meals. This dish
has been inspired by a French oven-baked omelette. To speed things up,
the recipe has been adapted for cooking on the hob. Serve with some
crusty bread and a salad.

1 Beat the eggs with some seasoning and 2 tablespoons of water. Set
aside.

2 Heat a medium-size heavy-based non-stick pan and when quite hot,
add the oil. Then add the onion, peppers and garlic. Stir-fry for about 7
minutes until softened, then stir in the tomato and seasoning.

3 Cook for about 3 minutes until the tomato softens and then stir in
the basil.

4 Pour in the eggs and allow to set on the bottom, then stir gently to
scramble lightly. Cover and cook gently until the top is nearly set and
then stir lightly again to slightly scramble. Serve immediately.

Serves 4

Points per serving 5
Total Points 19
Calories per serving 230

1 small cauliflower, cut into florets,
    reserving most of the stalk
1 head of broccoli, cut into florets,
    reserving most of the stalk
1 onion, sliced
1 vegetable stock cube
400 g (14 oz) canned kidney beans,
    drained
300 ml (10 fl oz) skimmed milk
1 tablespoon very-low-fat spread
3 tablespoons flour
a good pinch of dried mixed herbs
50 g (1¾ oz) grated fresh parmesan
    cheese
1–2 tablespoons natural colour dried
    breadcrumbs
1 large tomato, sliced
salt

Cauliflower and Broccoli Cheese

Ⓥ if vegetarian cheese is used • Freezing recommended
• Preparation and cooking time: 30 minutes. Buy some fresh ready-grated parmesan for the best flavour and to save time.

1 Bring a large pan of water to the boil, add salt to taste and boil the vegetable florets with the onion for 5–7 minutes, depending on how tender you like them.

2 Drain the vegetables but reserve 200 ml (7 fl oz) of the water and dissolve the stock cube in this. Place the vegetables into a shallow heat-proof dish. Sprinkle the canned beans of your choice over the cooked vegetables.

3 Preheat the grill to a medium high heat. Put the stock into a medium saucepan. Add the milk, very-low-fat spread, flour and herbs. Bring to the boil, whisking until smooth and creamy. Simmer for a minute, then remove and stir in three-quarters of the cheese.

4 Pour the sauce over the vegetables and pulses. Mix the remaining cheese with the breadcrumbs and sprinkle on top.

5 Arrange the tomato slices on top of the breadcrumb topping as a garnish and then grill until the top is golden brown and crispy. Serve hot.

Weight Watcher's note: If you replace the kidney beans with chick-peas, the Points will be the same.

Menu Plan

Breakfast		Lunch		Dinner	
½ medium Galia melon 250 g (9 oz)		2 medium slices toast	2 Points	Mushroom Pasties	
	1 Point	Small can 205 g (7 oz) baked beans		(1 serving) page 90	2 Points
Crumpet	1 Point		2 Points	2 tablespoons cold cooked rice	
2 teaspoons low-fat spread	1 Point	Small banana and an apple	1½ Points		1½ Points
				Large mixed salad	0 Points
				2 tablespoons reduced-calorie coleslaw	
					1 Point
				Large portion 120 g (4½ oz) sweetcorn	
					½ Point
				Medium portion 150 g (5½ oz)	
				strawberries	½ Point

Throughout the day: 1 pint skimmed milk 2 Points   **Treat:** Jam doughnut 4 Points

Lentil-stuffed Tomatoes

4 x 125 g (4½ oz) large ripe tomatoes

50 g (1¾ oz) macaroni or 150 g (5½ oz)
   cooked or leftover pasta

1 large salad onion, chopped

1 teaspoon garlic purée

400 g (14 oz) canned lentils, drained

2 teaspoons dried mixed herbs

1 tablespoon soy sauce or brown sauce

50 g (1¾ oz) half-fat Cheddar cheese,
   grated

salt and freshly ground black pepper

V if vegetarian cheese is used • Freezing not recommended • Preparation time: 20 minutes + 20–25 minutes cooking. Stuffed tomatoes make a wonderful treat.

1 Preheat the oven to Gas Mark 5/190°C/375°F. Cut the tops off the tomatoes and scoop out the flesh using a teaspoon. Chop the flesh, lightly season the insides of the shells and drain the hollow tomatoes upside down in a colander while you make the rest of the filling.

2 Boil the macaroni for 10 minutes and then drain (unless you are using cooked pasta). Mix the cooked pasta with the tomato flesh, onion, garlic, lentils, herbs, sauce of your choice and cheese.

3 Season and spoon into the tomato shells. Place the tops on the tomatoes and place on a small baking dish. Bake for about 20–25 minutes until the shells just start to soften and the filling is piping hot.

Braised Celery Hearts with Butter Beans

3 ready-trimmed celery hearts

1 onion, sliced thinly

400 g (14 oz) canned chopped tomatoes

½ teaspoon dried mixed herbs

425 g (15 oz) canned butter beans,
   drained

a little chopped fresh parsley (optional)

salt and freshly ground black pepper

V Freezing recommended • Preparation time: 10 minutes + 20 minutes cooking. Celery has such a lovely, distinctive flavour which goes so well with butter beans. Try this as a side dish when you want a change.

1 Put the celery hearts into a medium-size saucepan, making sure that they lie flat on the base. Scatter over the onion slices.

2 Tip in the tomatoes, herbs and seasoning, then bring to the boil. Cover and simmer gently for 20 minutes.

3 Mix in the butter beans and cook for another 5 minutes. Serve hot with parsley sprinkled over the top, if using.

Lentil-stuffed Tomatoes

Aubergine and Tofu in a Sweet and Sour Sauce *(page 102)*

Serves 4

Points per serving 5

Total Points 21

Calories per serving 135

3 carrots, cut into thick sticks

2 large parsnips, cut into thick sticks

1 large leek, sliced

½ vegetable stock cube

200 ml (7 fl oz) skimmed milk

2 tablespoons flour

2 teaspoons low-fat spread

2 tablespoons dried breadcrumbs

1 tablespoon grated low-fat cheese

salt

Carrot and Parsnip Bake

**Ⓥ if vegetarian cheese is used • Freezing recommended
• Preparation and cooking time: 40 minutes.** Carrots and parsnips are among our best-loved root vegetables. Not only do they taste wonderful together, they also go well with another favourite, leeks. They are all delicious baked in this light sauce. Baked potatoes are also good on the side.

1 Bring about 600 ml (1 pint) of lightly salted water to the boil and cook the carrots and parsnips for 5 minutes. Add the leek and cook for a further 3 minutes.

2 Drain, reserving about 200 ml (7 fl oz) of the vegetable water and dissolve the stock cube in it. Preheat the grill.

3 Put the vegetables into a shallow heatproof dish. Return the vegetable stock to the pan along with the milk and then stir in the flour and low-fat spread. Bring to the boil slowly, stirring until thickened and smooth. Preheat the grill to a medium high heat.

4 Pour the sauce over the vegetables. Mix the crumbs with the cheese and scatter over the top. Place under the grill and cook until lightly browned.

Serves 4

Points per serving 3

Total Points 11

Calories per serving 185

1 tablespoon sunflower oil

1 onion, sliced

200 g (7 oz) bag of ready-washed spinach leaves

1 teaspoon mild or medium curry powder

400 g (14 oz) canned chick-peas, drained

300 g (10½ oz) canned new potatoes, drained (halved if large)

salt and freshly ground black pepper

Spicy Chick-peas with Potatoes and Spinach

Ⓥ Freezing not recommended • Preparation and cooking time: 10 minutes. Serve this quick, wholesome meal with basmati rice and some low-fat plain yogurt drizzled over the top. Don't forget to add the extra Points.

1 Heat a large non-stick wok until hot, add the oil and then stir-fry the onion for 2 minutes. Toss in the spinach and stir until it wilts.

2 Mix in the curry powder, cook for a few seconds and then add the chick-peas and potatoes.

3 Season and cook for 2 minutes until piping hot.

Serves 4

Points per serving 6
Total Points 25
Calories per serving 280

300 g (10½ oz) young spinach leaves,
    washed
1 teaspoon oil
3 tablespoons dried breadcrumbs
25 g (1 oz) low-fat spread
50 g (1¾ oz) flour
400 ml (14 fl oz) skimmed milk
50 g (1¾ oz) grated fresh parmesan
    cheese
a little freshly grated nutmeg
4 large free-range eggs (at room
    temperature), separated
salt and freshly ground black pepper

Spinach Soufflé

v if vegetarian cheese is used • **Freezing recommended**
• **Preparation time: 30 minutes + 40 minutes cooking.** Fresh spinach
is much more of a pleasure to cook with now that you can buy it
ready-prepared. This is just as well since it is so healthy and delicious.
A soufflé is actually quite easy to make and can be prepared ahead and
then baked when the family come in. Just make sure that they are all
sitting down to eat when it is ready or it will surely sink!

1 Cook the spinach according to the pack instructions. Drain
thoroughly in a colander, using the back of a ladle to press down on the
spinach and remove excess water.
2 Set the spinach aside to cool.
3 Brush the inside of a 1.3 litre (2½ pint) soufflé dish or deep ovenproof dish with the oil (no need to brush the base), then sprinkle in the
breadcrumbs and shake them around the sides to coat. This will help
give the soufflé mixture something to hold on to as it rises.
4 If baking the soufflé now, preheat the oven to Gas Mark
4/180°C/350°F. Chop the cooled spinach finely.
5 Put the low-fat spread, flour, milk and seasoning into a saucepan
and bring to the boil, stirring constantly until the mixture thickens and
is smooth. Simmer for a minute, then add the chopped spinach and
cheese and add nutmeg to taste. Stir well to combine. Remove and cool
slightly.
6 Beat in the egg yolks. Whisk the egg whites until they form soft but
firm peaks. Using a large metal spoon, carefully fold in the egg whites
using a figure of eight motion. Spoon into the prepared dish.
7 Using a knife, make the top of the mixture level and then bake for
about 40 minutes until risen. Don't overbake; the top should be very
slightly wobbly and the centre creamy. Serve at once.

Cook's note: You can also prepare the soufflé up to stage 6 and bake
later. You could do this in the morning and then keep the mixture in
the fridge until you are ready to serve.

Serves **4**	Points per serving 2 Total Points 8½ Calories per serving 185

1 tablespoon olive or sunflower oil

1 onion, sliced

2 garlic cloves, crushed

1 red or yellow pepper, de-seeded and
    chopped

1 green pepper, de-seeded and chopped

1 aubergine, chopped into chunks

1 large courgette, sliced

400 g (14 oz) canned chopped tomatoes

1 teaspoon dried mixed herbs or 2
    tablespoons chopped fresh basil

4 free-range eggs, hard-boiled, peeled and
    quartered

salt and freshly ground black pepper

Ratatouille with Eggs

V **Freezing recommended** • **Preparation and cooking time: 30 minutes.** Hard-boiled eggs turn ratatouille into a delicious and satisfying main meal.

1 Heat the oil in a large frying-pan or wok and when hot, stir-fry the onion, garlic, peppers and aubergine for about 5 minutes until softened.

2 Add the courgette and cook for another 5 minutes. Stir in the tomatoes and dried herbs, if using. (If using fresh basil, add it at the next stage.) Season, bring to the boil, cover and simmer for 10 minutes.

3 If using fresh basil, mix in now and cook for a minute or two longer. Serve garnished with the egg quarters.

Cook's note: A ratatouille tastes best if the flavours are allowed to mellow overnight.

Serves **2**	Points per serving 3 Total Points 5½ Calories per serving 170

100 g (3½ oz) whole green or runner
    beans, topped and tailed, cut into
    chunks

200 g (7 oz) canned butter beans, drained

For the sauce:

100 g (3½ oz) button mushrooms, sliced

a good pinch of dried thyme

1 tablespoon light soy sauce (optional)

1 tablespoon flour

2 teaspoons low-fat spread

300 ml (10 fl oz) skimmed milk

salt and freshly ground black pepper

Green and White Beans in Mushroom Sauce

V **Freezing recommended** • **Preparation and cooking time: 20 minutes.** You can serve this as a light lunch with baked potatoes. It's quite handy if you have vegetarians coming for dinner and you don't know what to feed them. Just add pasta! It is also good with roast lamb or chicken.

1 Boil the green or runner beans in salted water for 5 minutes. Drain and mix with the canned beans of your choice in a shallow dish.

2 Put the mushrooms into a small saucepan with 2 tablespoons of water, the thyme and the soy sauce, if using. Cover and simmer for 5 minutes until softened. Remove the mushrooms with a slotted spoon.

3 Put the flour, low-fat spread and milk into the saucepan along with the mushroom juices. Bring to the boil, whisking until smooth and creamy.

4 Return the mushrooms, season to taste and simmer for another minute then pour over the beans. Serve warm.

Weight Watcher's note: If you replace the butter beans with cannellini beans, the Points per serving will be the same.

Ratatouille with Eggs

Serves 4

Points per serving 1½

Total Points 7

Calories per serving 155

1 onion, chopped

1 fat garlic clove, crushed

1 carrot, grated coarsely

1 small celery stick, chopped

½ small green pepper, chopped

1 tablespoon olive or sunflower oil

100 g (3½ oz) split red lentils

400 g (14 oz) canned chopped tomatoes

2 tablespoons tomato purée

450 ml (16 fl oz) vegetable stock

1 teaspoon dried marjoram or oregano

salt and freshly ground black pepper

Red Lentil Pasta Sauce

Ⓥ **Freezing recommended • Preparation time: 20 minutes + 20 minutes cooking.** Split red lentils are wonderful because you can use them straight from the pack and they don't need any pre-soaking. Not only that, they are cheap and very nutritious. This sauce cooks even faster than a traditional Bolognese sauce. Make it ahead if you wish – the flavours will only improve. Serve with your choice of pasta.

1 Put the onion, garlic, carrot, celery and green pepper into a large saucepan with the oil and 2 tablespoons of water. Mix together well and then heat until sizzling.

2 Cover and cook gently for 5 minutes. Then stir in the lentils, tomatoes, tomato purée, stock and marjoram or oregano. Bring to the boil, stirring, add some seasoning and then cover and simmer very gently for 15 minutes.

3 Uncover, stir, and cook for a few more minutes until the mixture has reduced and thickened.

Cauliflower and Broccoli Cheese *(page 93)*

Red Lentil Pasta Sauce

Menu Plan

Breakfast		Lunch		Dinner	
Small glass fruit juice	½ *Point*	15 cm (6-inch) slice French stick		Baked Bean Cobbler	
Medium slice toast, topped with			4½ *Points*	(1 serving) page 90	5½ *Points*
	1 *Point*	1 teaspoon low-fat spread	½ *Point*	Broccoli, leeks, green beans	0 *Points*
Small can tomatoes	0 *Points*	40 g (1½ oz) Cheddar cheese			
			4½ *Points*		
		Onion (or spring onions), tomato,			
		lettuce, cucumber	0 *Points*		
		Apple	½ *Point*		

Throughout the day: 1 pint skimmed milk *2 Points*   **Treat:** Small glass wine *1 Point*

Serves 4 — Points per serving 2 / Total Points 8 / Calories per serving 140

Aubergine and Tofu in a Sweet and Sour Sauce

1 small aubergine, cut into small chunks

2 large salad onions, cut into chunks

1 small red pepper, de-seeded and sliced thinly

1 tablespoon sunflower oil

200 g (7 oz) smoked or marinated tofu, cubed

salt and freshly ground black pepper

For the sauce:

2 tablespoons light soy sauce

2 tablespoons white wine vinegar

2 tablespoons light soft brown sugar

90 ml (3 fl oz) water

1 teaspoon cornflour

Ⓥ **Freezing not recommended • Preparation and cooking time: 20 minutes + 15 minutes salting.** Tofu is made of soya bean curd which is a high protein, low-fat food from China and Japan. It is very versatile and absorbs the flavour of the ingredients it is cooked with. Aubergines are great partners for tofu. Serve this dish with Thai rice or egg noodles.

1 If you have time, put the aubergine chunks into a colander and sprinkle with salt. Leave for 15 minutes to allow the bitter juices to seep out. Rinse well and pat dry with kitchen paper. This is not essential, but it does help to soften the aubergines so that they absorb less oil.

2 Mix all the vegetables together, including the aubergine, and toss well with the oil. Then stir-fry everything quickly in a hot wok for about 3 minutes. You may have to add a few tablespoons of water just to soften the vegetables a little more.

3 Now toss in the cubes of tofu and cook for another 1 or 2 minutes.

4 While the tofu is cooking, quickly stir together the sauce ingredients, mixing in the cornflour to make a smooth paste.

5 Toss the sauce into the vegetables and stir until thick and glossy. Check the seasoning and serve immediately.

Serves 4 — Points per serving 3 / Total Points 13 / Calories per serving 215

Mexican Stuffed Peppers

4 peppers, de-seeded and cored

1 onion, chopped

2 garlic cloves, crushed

1 tablespoon olive oil or sunflower oil

1 teaspoon ground coriander

1 teaspoon mild chilli powder

½ teaspoon ground cumin

½ teaspoon dried oregano

400 g (14 oz) canned chopped tomatoes

400 g (14 oz) red kidney beans, drained

2 tablespoons low-fat fromage frais

40 g (1½ oz) low-fat Cheddar cheese, grated

salt and freshly ground black pepper

Ⓥ **Freezing recommended • Preparation time: 20 minutes + 10 minutes cooking.** Garnish with coriander sprigs for a more Mexican look. Serve with rice.

1 Blanch the peppers in boiling water for 3–5 minutes until just soft but still holding their shape. Then drain the peppers upside-down in a colander.

2 Put the onion, garlic, oil, spices and oregano into a saucepan and heat until they all start to sizzle. Cover and cook gently for 5 minutes, shaking the pan occasionally.

3 Uncover and stir in the tomatoes and beans. Season and bring to the boil, then simmer uncovered for 10 minutes until reduced.

4 Stand the pepper shells on a serving platter and spoon in the filling. Stir the fromage frais until runny and then trickle over the peppers. Put small mounds of grated cheese on top of each pepper and serve hot.

Pasta
Pizza and Rice

Chapter 8

Everyone loves pasta and pizza, and rice dishes such as risotto or pilaff are also extremely popular. Believe it or not, as long as you avoid sauces which are high in Points and Calories, they make superb diet food and are good for you too. Pasta, rice and breads have long been the basis of healthy, balanced diets. This is because they are complex carbohydrates which are low in fat and full of slow-release energy which keeps our bodies going for longer than something like sugar which only gives us a quick fix of energy.

These recipes are very tasty indeed and you're sure to make them over and over again. For pizza lovers, there are quick pizzas which can be put together in 10 minutes when you are feeling pressured for time. If you're in the mood for some quick and tasty pasta, try the superb Pasta Puttanesca or 'harlot's pasta' which is spicy and satisfying. And don't miss out on the fabulous rice dishes such as Spicy Mince and Basmati Pilaff with the naturally fragrant basmati rice.

Points per serving 2½

Total Points 9

Calories per serving 235

200 g (7 oz) pasta bows

200 g (7 oz) young leaf spinach

100 g (3½ oz) low-fat soft cheese with
    garlic and herbs

2 tablespoons light soy sauce

a little freshly grated nutmeg

salt and freshly ground black pepper

Pasta Bows with Garlic and Spinach Sauce

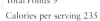 Freezing recommended • Preparation and cooking time: 15 minutes. This would be an excellent accompaniment for chops, grilled chicken or oven-baked mushrooms.

1 Boil the pasta in salted water according to the pack instructions. Drain, reserving about 150 ml (5 fl oz) of the cooking water in the pan.

2 Cook the spinach according to the pack instructions or lightly blanch in a little boiling water for 2–3 minutes. Drain well, then chop roughly.

3 Add the cheese to the pan with the pasta water and heat gently to melt. Then stir in the pasta, chopped spinach, soy sauce, nutmeg and seasoning. Reheat and serve.

Serves 4

Points per serving 10

Total Points 41

Calories per serving 550

500 g (1 lb 2 oz) lean minced beef

1 tablespoon sunflower oil

1 onion, chopped

2 garlic cloves, crushed or 2 teaspoons
    garlic purée

1 green pepper, de-seeded and chopped
    (optional)

1–2 teaspoons mild chilli powder

1 teaspoon ground cumin

½ teaspoon dried oregano

200 g (7 oz) easy-cook long-grain rice

400 g (14 oz) canned chopped tomatoes

2 tablespoons tomato purée

500 ml (18 fl oz) beef, chicken or
    vegetable stock

400 g (14 oz) canned red kidney beans or
    pinto beans, drained

salt and freshly ground black pepper

Chilli Con Carne Rice

Freezing recommended • Preparation and cooking time: 30 minutes. This pilaff-style dish of chilli mince, rice and beans is cheap, cheerful and simple to put together.

1 Heat a large non-stick frying-pan and when hot, stir-fry the mince with the oil for 2 minutes until browned and crumbly.

2 Add the onion, garlic and green pepper, if using, and cook for 5 minutes. Then stir in the spices and oregano.

3 Cook for a minute, then stir in the rice, chopped tomatoes, purée, stock and beans. Bring to the boil, season and stir. Then cover and cook on a gentle simmer for 15 minutes. Serve hot.

Variation: If you replace the minced beef with turkey, the Points per serving will be 8½ and if you use pork the Points per serving will be 9.

Serves (4)
Points per serving 5½
Total Points 22
Calories per serving 320

Italian Rice Soup with Ham and Peas

Freezing not recommended • **Preparation and cooking time: 30 minutes.** A really simple soupy risotto.

100 g (3½ oz) lean, thickly sliced honey roast ham, trimmed of all fat and cubed

1 onion, chopped

1 tablespoon olive oil

200 g (7 oz) risotto rice

1 litre (1¾ pints) hot vegetable or chicken stock (made with 2 stock cubes)

a pinch of sugar

250 g (9 oz) frozen peas

4 teaspoons grated fresh parmesan cheese

salt and freshly ground black pepper

1 Put the ham into a large saucepan with the onion and oil.

2 Heat until sizzling and cook on a medium heat for about 3 minutes, stirring once or twice.

3 Stir in the rice and cook for a minute, then add a quarter of the hot stock and stir frequently until absorbed.

4 Add another 2 ladlefuls of stock and stir often until absorbed. Repeat this until nearly all the stock is gone.

5 Stir in the sugar and peas. Bring the mixture back to the boil and then add the last of the stock. Cook for about 3 to 5 minutes until the rice is tender. Season to taste.

6 If the rice feels too firm, simply add a little boiling water. The total cooking time should be about 18 to 20 minutes. Serve immediately sprinkled with parmesan cheese.

Serves (4)
Points per serving 3
Total Points 11½
Calories per serving 285

Pasta Puttanesca

Freezing not recommended • **Preparation and cooking time: 10 minutes.** Pasta with a punch! Puttanesca sauce is a deliciously spicy way to pep up pasta.

50 g (1¾ oz) canned anchovies, 1 tablespoon of the oil reserved

2 garlic cloves, crushed or 2 teaspoons garlic purée

1 small onion, thinly sliced

1 fresh red chilli, de-seeded and chopped or 1–2 teaspoons red chilli paste or ½ teaspoon dried chilli flakes

400 g (14 oz) canned chopped tomatoes

½ teaspoon dried oregano

200 g (7 oz) pasta of your choice e.g. penne or conchiglie or tagliatelle

8 black olives, stoned and sliced

freshly ground black pepper

1 Dry the anchovies well with kitchen paper. Separate them into fillets and chop roughly.

2 Put the anchovies, the tablespoon of reserved anchovy oil, garlic, onion and chilli into a saucepan and cook over a medium heat for 5 minutes until softened and the anchovies have dissolved. The amount of chilli you add is your choice.

3 Stir in the chopped tomatoes, oregano and black pepper. Bring to the boil, then turn down to a simmer for 5 minutes.

4 Meanwhile, boil the pasta according to the pack instructions and drain, leaving slightly wet. Tip back into the saucepan.

5 Check the sauce for seasoning and add the olives. Reheat for a minute or so and then toss into the pasta. Serve immediately.

Serves 4

Points per serving 4½
Total Points 18½
Calories per serving 310

Risotto Primavera

- 250 g (9 oz) selection of fresh young tender vegetables e.g. baby carrots, baby corn, mange-tout peas, beans, button mushrooms, asparagus tips, cut into bite-size pieces
- 1 tablespoon olive oil
- 1 onion, chopped
- 2 garlic cloves, crushed or 2 teaspoons garlic purée
- 250 g (9 oz) risotto rice
- 3 tablespoons dry white wine (optional)
- 1.2 litres (2 pints) hot vegetable or chicken stock (made with 2 stock cubes)
- 25 g (1 oz) grated fresh parmesan cheese
- salt and freshly ground black pepper

Ⓥ if vegetarian cheese is used • Freezing not recommended • Preparation and cooking time: 35 minutes. 'Primavera' means spring in Italian, and refers to the young seasonal vegetables in this recipe.

1 Heat the oil to a medium heat in a large saucepan and gently sauté the onion and garlic for 5 minutes.

2 Stir in the rice and cook for a minute. Then add the wine (if using) and stir until absorbed.

3 Pour in a quarter of the hot stock and stir frequently for about 3 minutes until it is all absorbed. (Stirring a risotto is very important because it brings out the natural creaminess of the grain.)

4 Add any firm vegetables such as carrots. Continue adding stock in ladlefuls, stirring each amount until it is absorbed. You don't have to stir all the time, just often.

5 As you add more stock, add more of the vegetables but leave tender ones such as mushrooms or asparagus, which only take a few minutes to cook, until near the end.

6 The risotto will be ready after about 18 minutes cooking, by which time you should have added all the stock. If you want the rice to be more tender, then add extra boiling water. Season well and serve as soon as it is creamy, topped with the parmesan cheese.

Pasta Puttanesca (page 105)
Risotto Primavera

Menu Plan

Breakfast		Lunch		Dinner	
Small glass fruit juice	½ Point	Low-fat cooking spray		Pasta Bows with Garlic and Spinach	
Medium slice toast with melted		2 egg mushroom omelette	3 Points	Sauce (1 serving) page 104	
	1 Point	2 tablespoons peas	1 Point		2½ Points
Low-fat cheese slice, topped with		1 thick slice wholemeal bread		Medium chicken breast, grilled	
	1 Point		1½ Points		2¼ Points
Tomato slices	0 Points	1 teaspoon low-fat spread	½ Point	Large portion 120 g (4¼ oz) sweetcorn	
		Peach or nectarine	½ Point		½ Point
				Small banana sliced into	1 Point
				Small tub low-fat plain yogurt	
					1½ Points

Throughout the day: ½ pint skimmed milk *1 Point*   Treat: 25 g (1 oz) bag low-fat crisps any flavour *2 Points*

Nasi Goreng

1 egg, beaten

3 tablespoons light soy sauce

2 teaspoons sunflower oil

250 g (9 oz) lean minced beef

2 garlic cloves, crushed or 2 teaspoons
garlic purée

1 fresh red chilli, de-seeded and chopped
or 1–2 teaspoons red chilli paste

1 small green pepper, de-seeded and
chopped

2 teaspoons mild curry powder

1 teaspoon ground paprika

4 salad onions, sliced

200 g (7 oz) Thai jasmine or basmati rice

600 ml (1 pint) hot stock (any sort)

2 tablespoons tomato purée

salt and freshly ground black pepper

**Freezing recommended • Preparation time: 15 minutes + 30
minutes cooking.** A popular Indonesian dish of spicy rice and minced
beef topped with eggy strips. A quick one-pot meal which is tasty with
a crisp green salad tossed in a spicy salad dressing.

1 Beat the egg together with 2 teaspoons of soy sauce. Heat half a
teaspoon of the oil in a small frying-pan and when hot add the egg and
cook to make a flat, firm omelette. Remove, pat dry with kitchen paper,
then roll up and cut into strips. Set aside.

2 In a large saucepan, heat the remaining oil and brown the mince,
stirring well until nice and crumbly. Then stir in the garlic, chilli and
green pepper.

3 Cook for 3 minutes, then mix in the curry powder and paprika.
Cook for a minute, then add three of the onions, all the rice, the stock,
tomato purée, remaining soy sauce and seasoning.

4 Bring to the boil, stirring and then cover and cook very gently for 12
minutes without lifting the lid. Remove from the heat, still covered and
leave to stand for 5 minutes.

5 Fork the rice gently and pile up into a mound on a serving platter.
Garnish with the egg strips and remaining onion.

Penne with Fresh Tomatoes and Basil

100 g (3½ oz) penne or any other pasta
shape

2 fresh tomatoes

2 teaspoons olive oil (preferably extra-
virgin)

1 garlic clove, crushed, or 1 teaspoon
garlic purée

3 large leaves of fresh basil, torn

salt and freshly ground black pepper

Ⓥ **Freezing not recommended • Preparation and cooking time:
15–20 minutes.** When time is short and you need a fresh-tasting light
meal, nothing beats a plate of pasta tossed in a tasty, light sauce. If you
can, use extra-virgin olive oil; because it is so aromatic, you don't need
to use as much for a great flavour.

1 Cook the pasta in plenty of boiling water according to the pack
instructions.

2 Meanwhile, score a cross at the top of each tomato and dip them
into the pasta water for half a minute, using a slotted spoon. Remove
and peel off the skin – it should be easy to slip off now.

3 Chop the tomatoes, discarding the cores. Drain the pasta when it is
ready but leave it slightly wet.

4 Return the pasta to the pan and add the oil. Stir in the chopped
tomatoes and garlic. Stir for a minute or two until hot and add the
basil. Season to taste and serve immediately.

700 ml (1¼ pints) skimmed milk
200 g (7 oz) semolina
1 tablespoon low-fat spread
50 g (1¾ oz) grated fresh parmesan
    cheese
a little freshly grated nutmeg
1 large egg, beaten and seasoned
300 g (10½ oz) fresh young spinach
400 g (14 oz) canned chopped tomatoes
    with garlic or herbs
salt and freshly ground black pepper

Spinach and Tomato Gnocchi

**Ⓥ if vegetarian cheese is used • Freezing recommended •
Preparation time: 35 minutes + 25 minutes baking.** An inexpensive
and nourishing family dish from Italy.

1 Heat the milk in a large non-stick saucepan, until it reaches the
boiling point and then turn down to a simmer and slowly pour in the
semolina, beating well with a wooden spoon until smooth.
2 Simmer gently for 2 minutes and then remove from the heat. Beat in
the low-fat spread, three-quarters of the cheese, the nutmeg and
seasoning. Cool and then beat in the egg.
3 Spoon the mixture into a clean shallow dish or tray and spread to a
thickness of 1 cm (½ inch). Leave to set and cool. Cut into 2.5 cm
(1-inch) squares.
4 Preheat the oven to Gas Mark 5/190°C/375°F. Meanwhile, cook the
spinach according to the pack instructions if it comes ready-washed.
Otherwise, wash well, drain and cook in a covered pan without extra
water until limp. Drain well, squashing it down with the back of a ladle
to remove any excess water. Season and chop roughly.
5 Place the spinach in the base of a shallow ovenproof dish, then
spoon over the chopped tomatoes. Season again, arrange the gnocchi
squares on top and sprinkle with the remaining cheese. Bake for
25–30 minutes until golden brown and crispy on top.

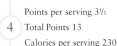

250 g (9 oz) basmati rice or long-grain rice
    (not easy-cook)
½ teaspoon salt
1 cinnamon stick
1 large bay leaf
3–4 whole cloves
3–4 green cardamoms
1 teaspoon low-fat spread

Whole Spice Pilaff

**Ⓥ Freezing not recommended • Preparation and cooking time: 25
minutes.** Make sure no-one eats the whole spices!

1 In a sieve, rinse the rice under a cold running tap for about a
minute, then drain.
2 Put the rice and 500 ml (18 fl oz) water into a medium-size
saucepan with a well-fitting lid. Bring to the boil and then stir in the
salt and all the spices.
3 Turn the heat right down to a gentle simmer, clamp on the lid and
cook for 10 minutes without lifting the lid. It is important not to let
out any steam.
4 Remove from the heat, still covered, and leave to stand for 5
minutes. Then uncover and gently fork through the low-fat spread.

Serves (4) Points per serving 5½
Total Points 21
Calories per serving 325

400 g (14 oz) smoked haddock or cod
1 large bay leaf
200 g (7 oz) basmati or long-grain rice
1 onion, chopped
2 teaspoons low-fat spread
1 teaspoon mild curry powder
2 free-range eggs, hard-boiled and chopped
3 tablespoons low-fat fromage frais
2 tablespoons chopped fresh parsley
     (optional)
a few pinches of cayenne pepper or a few
     drops of hot pepper sauce (optional)
salt and freshly ground black pepper

Kedgeree

Ⓥ see Cook's note • **Freezing not recommended** • **Preparation and cooking time: 1 hour.** This is a great British favourite. For the best flavour, use basmati rice and cook it in the fish poaching water.

1 Place the fish in a wide saucepan and pour over 500 ml (18 fl oz) boiling water. Add the bay leaf, return to the boil and then turn down to a very gentle simmer. Cook for 5 minutes or until the fish is just beginning to flake.

2 Remove the fish using a fish slice and strain the liquid into a jug. Put aside for use later. Skin and flake the fish and check well for any stray bones.

3 Under cold running water, rinse the rice in a sieve for about a minute and then drain. Add the onion and the low-fat spread to the saucepan which the fish was cooked in. Heat until sizzling, stir and lower the heat to a gentle sauté.

4 Cook for 5 minutes, stir in the curry powder, wait a few seconds and then stir in the rice and the reserved fish water. Add ½ teaspoon salt and some black pepper to taste.

5 Bring to the boil, stir once, and then cover and cook very gently for 10 minutes without lifting the lid. Remove from the heat, still covered, and leave to stand for 5 minutes.

6 Gently add the flaked fish, eggs and fromage frais by forking them through and reheat. Mix the parsley and hot pepper sauce, or cayenne pepper, if using, into the kedgeree. Serve piping hot.

Spaghetti with Spicy Prawn Sauce *(page 112)*
Kedgeree

Cook's note: Vegetarians can make a kedgeree by using vegetable stock to cook the rice and substituting a can of lentils for the fish.

Menu Plan

Breakfast		Lunch		Dinner	
Small glass fruit juice	*½ Point*	2 cream crackers and 2 Ryvita	*1 Point*	**Nasi Goreng**	
Egg, scrambled	*1½ Points*	Small tub 115 g (4 oz) diet cottage		(1 serving) page 108	*6 Points*
Medium slice toast	*1 Point*	cheese with chives	*1½ Points*	Mini pitta bread	*1 Point*
1 teaspoon low-fat spread	*½ Point*	Pickled onions, baby tomatoes	*0 Points*	Salad	*0 Points*
Sliced tomato	*0 Points*	Apple and 2 satsumas or tangerines		Fat-free salad dressing	*0 Points*
			1 Point	1 meringue nest filled with	*1 Point*
				Medium portion 150 g (5½ oz)	
				strawberries	*½ Point*

Throughout the day: 1 pint skimmed milk *2 Points*   **Treat:** Cadbury's Flake *2½ Points*

Serves **4**

Points per serving 4½

Total Points 17½

Calories per serving 145

1 onion, chopped

2 garlic cloves, crushed, or 2 teaspoons garlic purée

2 teaspoons olive oil or sunflower oil

3 tablespoons dry vermouth or 100 ml (3½ fl oz) dry white wine (optional)

400 g (14 oz) canned chopped tomatoes

½ teaspoon dried oregano

200 g (7 oz) spaghetti

200 g (7 oz) peeled prawns, thawed if frozen

2 tablespoons half-fat crème fraîche

salt and freshly ground black pepper

Spaghetti with Spicy Prawn Sauce

Freezing not recommended • **Preparation and cooking time: 40 minutes.** If you use quick-cook spaghetti for this dish, make sure you don't overcook it. For the best flavour, choose Atlantic prawns.

1 Put the onion, garlic and oil into a medium saucepan and stir well. Heat until sizzling, then add 2 tablespoons of water, cover and sauté very gently for 5 minutes until softened.

2 Add the vermouth or wine, if using, and cook until reduced by half, then stir in the chopped tomatoes, oregano and seasoning. Bring to the boil, then simmer for 10 minutes.

3 Meanwhile, boil the spaghetti according to the pack instructions, then drain but leave slightly wet by tipping straight back into the pan.

4 Add the prawns and crème fraîche to the pan, reheat, check the seasoning and toss into the spaghetti. Serve at once.

Variation: If you add 200 g (7 oz) clams in brine, it will give you a dish similar to the classic Italian Spaghetti alla Vongole.

Serves **4**

Points per serving 5½

Total Points 21½

Calories per serving 335

2 teaspoons olive oil or sunflower oil

2 lean back bacon rashers, trimmed of fat and chopped

150 g (5½ oz) skinless, boneless chicken, chopped

1 onion, chopped

2 garlic cloves, crushed, or 2 teaspoons garlic purée

1 small red pepper, de-seeded and chopped

1 tablespoon paprika

1 teaspoon turmeric

2 teaspoon dried marjoram

200 g (7 oz) risotto rice

850 ml (1½ pints) chicken stock

125 g (4½ oz) frozen peas, thawed

salt and freshly ground black pepper

Quick and Easy Paella

Freezing not recommended • **Preparation and cooking time: 45 minutes.** It is important to use the right sort of rice in a paella – one which will be creamy and yet still retain some bite. Buying authentic paella rice is not easy, but Italian arborio rice is a good substitute.

1 Heat the oil in a large non-stick frying-pan. When quite hot, stir-fry the bacon and chicken for about 2 minutes, then add the onion, garlic and red pepper.

2 Continue cooking for about 3 minutes, stirring occasionally and then mix in the spices, marjoram and rice. Cook for a minute.

3 Pour in all the stock and bring to the boil, stirring well. It will look very wet, but don't worry – risotto rice absorbs a lot of liquid. Add seasoning to taste and then turn the heat down to a simmer. Cover and cook gently for about 15 minutes. While it is cooking, either stir or shake the pan once only.

4 Add the peas and return to cook for another 3 minutes.

5 Allow to stand, covered and off the heat, for 5 minutes.

Quick and Easy Paella

Serves 4

Points per serving 7½
Total Points 29
Calories per serving 470

Tuna Noodle Bake

250 g (9 oz) pasta e.g. tagliatelle
200 g (7 oz) canned tuna in brine, drained
    and flaked
1 tablespoon low-fat spread
1 onion, chopped
1 celery stick, sliced thinly (optional)
1 large red, green or yellow pepper,
    de-seeded and chopped
2 x 285 g cans of Weight Watchers from
    Heinz Mushroom Soup
300 ml (10 fl oz) skimmed milk
1 tablespoon cornflour
200 g (7 oz) canned sweetcorn
½ teaspoon dried mixed herbs or oregano
50 g (1¾ oz) Edam cheese, grated
salt and freshly ground black pepper

Freezing recommended • Preparation and cooking time: 25 minutes. Everyone loves a creamy tuna and pasta dish.

1 Boil the pasta according to the pack instructions. Then drain, rinse in cold water and leave in the colander. Flake the tuna and set aside.
2 Put the low-fat spread, onion, celery and red, green or yellow pepper into the saucepan you have just used to cook the pasta and heat until the contents start to sizzle. Add 3 tablespoons of water, cover and cook over a gentle heat for 5 minutes.
3 Stir in all of the soup and start to heat. Blend a little of the milk with the cornflour and add this to the pan along with the rest of the milk, the corn and the herbs.
4 Bring to the boil, stirring until smooth, then cook for a minute. Mix in the tuna and then finally stir in the pasta. Season to taste. Preheat the grill.
5 Tip the tuna and noodles into a shallow heatproof dish, sprinkle over the cheese and brown under the grill until hot and bubbling.

Serves 4

Points per serving 11
Total Points 44½
Calories per serving 405

Quick Cannelloni

2 teaspoons olive oil or sunflower oil
500 g (1 lb 2 oz) extra-lean minced beef
2 garlic cloves, crushed, or 2 teaspoons
    garlic purée
1 small red or yellow pepper, de-seeded
    and chopped finely
2 tablespoons tomato purée
1 tablespoon mild chilli relish (optional)
½ teaspoon dried mixed herbs
8 lasagne sheets, fresh or dried
200 g (7 oz) half-fat crème fraîche
4 teaspoons grated fresh parmesan cheese
salt and freshly ground black pepper

Freezing recommended • Preparation and cooking time: 30 minutes. Lasagne sheets wrapped around a quick-fried mince filling is a simple and delicious way to make cannelloni.

1 To make the filling, heat the oil in a large non-stick frying-pan and when it is quite hot, stir-fry the mince, stirring well to break up any lumps.
2 Add the garlic and chopped red or yellow pepper and continue to cook for 5 minutes. Then stir in the tomato purée, chilli relish, if using, and herbs. Season and add about 300 ml (½ pint) water.
3 Bring to the boil then simmer, uncovered, until the liquid has almost evaporated, stirring once or twice.
4 Meanwhile, if using dried lasagne sheets, boil them for about 7 minutes in plenty of boiling water, then drain and rinse in hot water. If using fresh lasagne, follow the pack instructions. Preheat the grill.
5 Divide the filling between the lasagne sheets and roll up. Place join-side down in a shallow heatproof dish.
6 Spoon the crème fraîche on top and sprinkle over the cheese. Grill until browned and bubbling.

Tuna Noodle Bake
Quick Cannelloni

French Bread Pizzas

46 cm (18-inch) long French bread stick

400 g (14 oz) canned chopped tomatoes

½ teaspoon dried mixed herbs

100 g (3½ oz) thinly sliced ham, cut into strips

200 g (7 oz) canned sweetcorn, drained

85 g (3 oz) Edam cheese, grated

freshly ground black pepper

Freezing not recommended • **Preparation and cooking time: 20 minutes.** These pizzas are easy, light and crisp.

1 Preheat the oven to Gas Mark 5/190°C/375°F. Cut the bread stick in half and then slit each half in half. Lay them on a baking sheet, lined up side by side.

2 Scatter over the chopped tomatoes, including the juice from the can, and then sprinkle with herbs. Divide the ham between the pizzas, scatter over the sweetcorn, season with pepper and finally, top with the cheese.

3 Bake for 10–20 minutes or until the cheese starts bubbling. Serve immediately.

Bacon and Onion Pizza

1 medium thin and crispy fresh pizza base

200 g (7 oz) canned chopped tomatoes

1 small red onion, sliced very finely

2 teaspoons pesto

4 rashers of lean back bacon, fat removed, cut into large pieces

200 g (7 oz) cooked potato, sliced thinly (optional)

2 teaspoons grated fresh parmesan cheese

salt and freshly ground black pepper

Freezing recommended • **Preparation and cooking time: 35 minutes.** Potato is very popular on pizza in Italy, especially with bacon, so if you want a truly Italian treat, make sure you use the potato.

1 Preheat the oven to Gas Mark 6/200°C/400°F. Lay the pizza base on a baking sheet.

2 Scatter over the chopped tomatoes, including the can juice. Then place the onion slices randomly on top and trickle over the pesto.

3 Put the bacon and potato slices, if using, on the pizzas. Sprinkle with the cheese and seasoning. Be generous with the pepper.

4 Bake for 15 minutes until the bacon is cooked and the onion lightly browned. Cool for 5 minutes and then cut into wedges to serve.

Weight Watcher's note: If using the potato, add 1 Point per serving.

Serves 4

Points per serving 4½

Total Points 18½

Calories per serving 310

100 g (3½ oz) macaroni

1 onion, chopped

2 garlic cloves, crushed or 2 teaspoons
    garlic purée

1 tablespoon olive oil or sunflower oil

1 teaspoon ground cumin

1 teaspoon ground coriander

100 g (3½ oz) easy-cook rice (ideally
    easy-cook basmati)

400 g (14 oz) canned chopped tomatoes

400 g (14 oz) canned lentils, can liquor
    reserved

2 tablespoons chopped fresh coriander or
    parsley

salt and freshly ground black pepper

Kastori

Ⓥ Freezing recommended • Preparation and cooking time: 30 minutes. It may sound strange, but rice and pasta do go well together in the same dish as you'll see in this Egyptian country dish with a mildly spicy tomato and lentil sauce.

1 Boil the macaroni according to the pack instructions. Drain and set aside.

2 Put the onion and garlic into a large saucepan with the oil. Heat until they start to sizzle, then sauté for 5 minutes. Stir in the spices and cook for a minute. Mix in the rice and cook for another minute.

3 Add the tomatoes, lentils (and can liquor) and 300 ml (10 fl oz) water. Season well, bring to the boil, then cover and simmer very gently for 15 minutes.

4 Stir in the cooked macaroni, fresh coriander or parsley, reheat and serve.

Serves 4

Points per serving 5

Total Points 21

Calories per serving 360

1 tablespoon olive oil or sunflower oil

2 medium skinless, boneless chicken
    breasts, cut into small cubes

2 leeks, sliced thinly

2 x 285 g cans of Weight Watchers from
    Heinz Chicken or Mushroom Soup

grated zest and juice of 1 lemon

1 tablespoon dry sherry (optional)

2 tablespoons half-fat crème fraîche

200 g (7 oz) pasta shells

2 tablespoons chopped fresh parsley

salt and freshly ground black pepper

Pasta Bows with Chicken and Lemon Sauce

Freezing recommended • Preparation and cooking time: 30 minutes. An economical and tasty way to cook chicken breasts.

1 Heat the oil in a non-stick saucepan and brown the chicken cubes for about 2 minutes, stirring. Add the leeks and cook for another 3 minutes.

2 Add the soup, lemon zest and sherry, if using. Season and bring to the boil, then simmer for about 10 minutes until reduced and the chicken is cooked.

3 Stir in the crème fraîche and reheat, then take the pan off the heat, add half the lemon juice and taste. If you would like more lemon juice, add the rest. Otherwise leave out.

4 Cook the pasta according to the pack instructions, drain and toss into the chicken sauce. Reheat, check the seasoning and serve hot sprinkled with the parsley.

Serves 4 | Points per serving 4½
Total Points 18½
Calories per serving 265

Creamy Mushroom Pasta

200 g (7 oz) pasta shapes e.g. farfalle

2 rashers of very lean back bacon,
de-rinded and chopped

2 teaspoons olive oil or sunflower oil

1 courgette, sliced

2 tablespoons light soy sauce

2 tablespoons dry vermouth or sherry
(optional)

250 g (9 oz) mushrooms e.g. button,
oyster or shiitake, sliced

½ teaspoon dried thyme

200 g (7 oz) very low-fat plain fromage
frais

salt and freshly ground black pepper

Freezing recommended • Preparation and cooking time: 25 minutes.
If you wish, include some oyster mushrooms or even a few sliced fresh shiitakes in this dish. Like their button mushroom cousins, they are very low in Points and Calories!

1 Boil the pasta according to the pack instructions. Drain and set aside.
2 Meanwhile, make the sauce. Cook the bacon in the oil in a large saucepan for 2 minutes, stirring well and then add the courgette and cook for another minute or two until softened.
3 Add the soy sauce, vermouth or sherry, if using, and 3 tablespoons of water to the pan. Stir in the mushrooms and thyme. Cover and cook for 3 minutes, shaking the pan occasionally.
4 Uncover and stir in the fromage frais. Reheat to just below boiling. Do not allow it to boil or it might curdle. Add the pasta, season and serve hot.

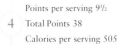

Serves 4 | Points per serving 9½
Total Points 38
Calories per serving 505

Spicy Mince and Basmati Pilaff

1 tablespoon sunflower oil

1 onion, chopped

2 garlic cloves, crushed or 2 tablespoons
garlic purée

1 teaspoon ginger purée or 2 teaspoons
ground ginger

500 g (1 lb 2 oz) lean beef mince

250 g (9 oz) easy-cook basmati and wild
rice or easy-cook basmati rice

2 teaspoons mild curry powder

850 ml (1½ pints) beef, chicken or
vegetable stock

125 g (4½ oz) frozen green beans

2 tablespoons chopped fresh coriander or
parsley (optional)

2 tablespoons low-fat plain yogurt

salt and freshly ground black pepper

Freezing not recommended • Preparation and cooking time: 40 minutes. An easy one-pot meal with a spicy and refreshing taste.

1 Heat the oil in a large saucepan and then sauté the onion, garlic and ginger for 5 minutes. Raise the heat and stir in the mince of your choice, stirring well to break up any lumps. Make sure the meat is crumbly.
2 Stir in the rice, then the curry powder and cook for a minute. Mix in the stock and seasoning. Bring to the boil, then cover and turn the heat right down to a simmer.
3 Cook for 15 minutes, then uncover and stir in the beans. Cover again and cook for a further 5 minutes. Take the pan off the heat and let stand, then gently fork through the herbs, if using. Serve topped with the yogurt.

Variation: Replace the beef with pork and deduct 1½ Points per serving, or use turkey and deduct 2 Points per serving.

Packed
Lunches

Chapter **9**

Many more of us are now eating at least one meal away from home every day which can play havoc with a diet if you're not careful since store-bought convenience foods can be very high in Points and Calories. They can also be quite hard on your budget since they are increasingly expensive; especially when you multiply the cost by 5 days. You're much better off making something at home which will save you Points and money.

So here are a few ideas which should inspire you to put together your own creations. And they are so delicious that you can really look forward to them for lunch!

Not only are these packed lunches healthy and low in Points, they will also save you time since some can be made ahead and frozen for later. Another idea for lunch is to make a soup from the soup chapter and pack it in a wide vacuum flask.

Serves **4**

Points per serving 4
Total Points 15½
Calories per serving 290

**200 g (7 oz) macaroni or small pasta
    shapes**
2 tablespoons fat-free French dressing
2 salad onions, chopped
2 carrots, grated coarsely
½ small red or yellow pepper, chopped finely
**2 tablespoons chopped fresh parsley or 1
    punnet of salad cress, snipped**
200 g (7 oz) canned sweetcorn, drained
100 g (3½ oz) lean ham, chopped
1 tablespoon low-calorie mayonnaise
2 tablespoons milk
salt and freshly ground black pepper

Ham and Pasta Pot

**Freezing not recommended • Preparation and cooking time: 20
minutes.** Small pasta shapes such as macaroni are best for a packed
lunch since they are easy to eat with a fork or a spoon.

1 Boil the macaroni according to the pack instructions, then drain and
toss with the French dressing. Season well and allow to cool while you
prepare the rest of the ingredients.

2 When the pasta is at room temperature, toss in the onions, carrots,
red or yellow pepper, parsley or snipped cress, sweetcorn and ham.

3 Beat the mayonnaise and milk together and mix in. Check the
seasoning and store chilled until required.

Serves **4**

Points per serving 2
Total Points 7½
Calories per serving 100

**85 g (3 oz) half-fat mature Cheddar, grated
    finely**
**200 g (7 oz) skimmed milk soft cheese
    e.g. quark**
**1 small bunch of chives or 2 salad onions,
    chopped very finely**
2 tablespoons chopped fresh parsley
1–2 teaspoons garlic purée (optional)
½ teaspoon coarsely ground black pepper
salt, to taste

Tangy Cheese Spread

Ⓥ if vegetarian cheese is used • Freezing recommended
  • **Preparation time: 10 minutes + chilling.**
This spread can turn a crispbread into a wonderful snack.

1 Beat the grated cheese with the soft cheese until smooth and then
mix in the chives or salad onions, parsley, garlic and pepper.

2 Season with salt and then spoon into a small food container and
chill until set.

Ham and Pasta Pot
Tabbouleh *(page 128)*

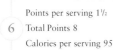

Serves 6

Points per serving 1½
Total Points 8
Calories per serving 95

Honey and Soy Chicken Drumsticks

6 chicken drumsticks, thawed well if frozen

a few pinches of sesame seeds (optional)

For the marinade:

2 tablespoons dark soy sauce

1 tablespoon dry sherry

1 teaspoon garlic purée or 2 teaspoons garlic powder

½ teaspoon Chinese five-spice powder (optional)

2 teaspoons clear honey

freshly ground black pepper

Freezing recommended if fresh chicken is used • Preparation time: 10 minutes + 1 hour marinating + 30 minutes cooking. These spicy drumsticks are something to look forward to for lunch!

1 Pull the skin off the drumsticks; it helps to hold the knuckle with a cloth as you tug. Pop the drumsticks into a food bag.

2 Mix all the marinade ingredients together in a jug, then pour the marinade into the food bag and rub well into the drumsticks. Leave to marinate for at least an hour.

3 Meanwhile, preheat the oven to Gas Mark 4/180°C/350°F. Tip the drumsticks on to a shallow roasting pan and bake for 30 minutes, turning occasionally until dark brown and glossy. Sprinkle over a few sesame seeds as they cool.

Serves 4

Points per serving 3½
Total Points 14
Calories per serving 110

Rose Marie Prawn Rolls

200 g (7 oz) peeled prawns, thawed if frozen (preferably North Atlantic)

2 tablespoons low-fat mayonnaise

2 tablespoons low-fat plain yogurt

1 tablespoon tomato ketchup

a big pinch of paprika

grated zest of 1 small lemon

1 teaspoon fresh lemon juice

4 small brown baps

4 crisp lettuce leaves

some snipped salad cress or a little chopped fresh parsley (optional)

salt and freshly ground black pepper

Freezing not recommended • Preparation time: 10 minutes + chilling. Prawn sandwiches are one of the most popular sandwich choices but the ones you buy are usually very high in Points and Calories. This home-made version not only tastes better, it's much lower in fat.

1 Pat the prawns dry with kitchen paper and then chop roughly. Mix with the mayonnaise, yogurt, ketchup, paprika, lemon zest and juice. Season to taste.

2 Open up the baps and line with lettuce. Spoon in the prawn filling and sprinkle over the cress or parsley, if using. Press together and wrap in clingfilm. Chill until ready to eat.

Rose Marie Prawn Rolls
B L T Pitta *(page 126)*

Serves **2**

Points per serving 4

Total Points 8

Calories per serving 230

2 medium free-range eggs

1 teaspoon reduced-calorie mayonnaise (for hard-boiled egg)

2 teaspoons light soy sauce (optional for scrambled egg)

1 teaspoon sunflower oil or olive oil (for scrambled egg)

4 medium slices of fresh brown or white bread

1 sliced tomato

2 tablespoons chopped prawns

salt and freshly ground black pepper

Choose from: 1 punnet salad cress; small bunch of watercress, stalks removed; 1 salad onion, chopped; shredded lettuce; a few thin slices of cucumber and radish

Tomato, Prawn and Egg Sandwich

Ⓥ **Freezing not recommended** • **Preparation time: 10 minutes.** You can make hard-boiled egg sandwiches or creamy, scrambled egg ones, and then choose the flavourings to suit.

1 If making hard-boiled egg filling, put the eggs in a small pan and cover with cold water. Bring to the boil and then cook for 8 minutes. Drain and run under cold water for 2 minutes. Peel and chop finely. Mix with the mayonnaise and seasoning. If making scrambled egg filling, beat the raw eggs with 2 teaspoons of soy sauce, if liked, and season. Heat the oil in a small non-stick pan and when really hot, swirl it around to coat the pan. Pour in the egg and stir often until lightly set and creamy. Tip out of the pan while still a little creamy – you don't want to overcook the egg.

2 Spread your egg filling on two slices of bread and top with the tomato slices, prawns and the additional filling(s) of your choice. Press the other slices of bread firmly on top and cut in four diagonally.

Weight Watchers note: All Points and Calories given are for sandwiches using the hard-boiled egg filling. If using the scrambled egg filling add a ¹/₂ Point per serving.

Serves **2**

Points per serving 3

Total Points 6¹/₂

Calories per serving 200

100 g (3¹/₂ oz) canned tuna in brine, drained and flaked

3 tablespoons sweetcorn, thawed if frozen, drained if canned

1 salad onion, chopped finely

1 tablespoon low-fat mayonnaise

4 medium slices of bread

freshly ground black pepper

Tuna and Corn Sandwich

Freezing not recommended • **Preparation time: 5 minutes.**

1 Simply mix together the first four ingredients, season and divide between two slices of bread. Top with another two slices.

Old English Cucumber or Tomato Sandwiches

Serves **2**

Points per serving 2½
Total Points 5
Calories per serving 120

¼ cucumber or 2 large ripe tomatoes
fine or flaked sea salt
4 medium slices of bread spread with 2
   teaspoons low-fat spread
freshly ground black pepper
For the topping, choose from:
a few leaves of watercress, chopped
a little chopped fresh dill or a pinch of
   dried dill
a little chopped fresh mint or parsley or
   chives or all 3
a few drops of wine vinegar

ⓥ **Freezing not recommended** • **Preparation time: 10 minutes + 20 minutes draining.** Lightly salting cucumber or tomato with sea salt gives them a lovely texture and flavour. If you want to serve truly old-style sandwiches, serve in triangles, with the crusts removed.

1 If using cucumbers, slice the cucumbers into wafer-thin rounds, leaving the skin on. If you have a food processor with a slicer, use this. Layer the cucumber rounds in a colander, sprinkling each layer lightly with salt. Leave to drain for 15–20 minutes. Don't rinse the cucumbers, simply pat them dry with kitchen paper.

2 Flavour the cucumber as desired by selecting ingredients from the 'choose from' list. Layer everything on 2 slices of bread. Season with pepper only. Make into sandwiches with the remaining two bread slices, remove the crusts, cut and serve.

3 If using tomatoes, to peel them, score a cross in the top of the tomatoes and then dip them in a pan of boiling water for just under a minute. Remove, cool under a cold running tap and then peel.

4 Cut out the cores and then slice as thinly as possible using a serrated knife. Divide the tomato slices between two slices of bread and season well. Sprinkle over the fresh herbs of your choice. Press two bread slices on top, remove the crusts, cut and serve.

Menu Plan

Breakfast		Lunch		Dinner	
50 g (1¾ oz) moist ready-to-eat		B L T Pittas		3 fish fingers, grilled	*3 Points*
apricots (approx. 10)	*1 Point*	(1 serving) page 126	*5½ Points*	Medium portion 200 g (7 oz) boiled	
Small tub low-fat plain yogurt		2 tablespoons reduced-calorie coleslaw		potatoes	*2 Points*
	1½ Points		*1 Point*	3 tablespoons baked beans	*1 Point*
		Apple and an orange	*1 Point*	Mushrooms and grilled tomatoes	
					0 Points
				Rhubarb, stewed with granulated	
				artificial sweetener	*0 Points*
				Small pot 150 g (5½ oz) low-fat ready-	
				to-serve custard	*2 Points*

Throughout the day: ½ pint skimmed milk *1 Point*   **Treat:** Small glass wine *1 Point*

Serves 2

Points per serving 4
Total Points 8
Calories per serving 310

1 large green pepper, de-seeded and
    quartered
1 large beef tomato, halved across the
    centre
a good pinch of dried oregano or basil
2 large Granary or wholemeal rolls or baps,
    split in half
100 g (3½ oz) reduced-fat hummous
a handful of fresh beanshoots or alfalfa
    sprouts
salt and freshly ground black pepper

Grilled Vegetable and Hummous Rolls

Ⓥ **Freezing not recommended** • **Preparation and cooking time: 20 minutes.** If you want to use the beansprouts, look for them in health food shops.

1 Preheat the grill to very hot. Place the pepper slices skin-side up and the tomato cut-side up on the grilling rack.

2 Sprinkle the tomato with the oregano or basil. Grill the vegetables until the pepper skins start to blacken and the tomatoes soften. Remove from the grill, cover the pepper skins with a clean tea towel for 5 minutes and then peel off the skin (or as much of it as you can).

3 Spread the roll halves with hummous. Divide the grilled vegetables between the rolls, add the fresh sprouts, if using, and season. Press the roll halves together, then wrap and cool.

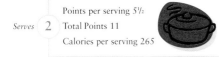

Serves 2

Points per serving 5½
Total Points 11
Calories per serving 265

4 lean back bacon rashers, trimmed of all
    fat
4 ripe tomatoes, sliced thinly
¼ iceberg lettuce
1 tablespoon low-fat French dressing
2 tablespoons low-fat plain yogurt
2 medium pitta breads, cut in half and
    opened as pockets
salt and freshly ground black pepper

B. L. T. Pittas

Freezing not recommended • **Preparation and cooking time: 15 minutes.** Everyone seems to love bacon, lettuce and tomato sandwiches but they are usually high in Points and Calories. Here are some lower-calorie ones to enjoy.

1 Grill the bacon for about 3 minutes until crisp, then pat dry with kitchen paper. Snip into pieces if you like, otherwise leave whole.

2 Season the tomato slices. Shred the lettuce, then season and mix with the dressing and yogurt.

3 Mix the bacon and tomato carefully into the lettuce and stuff into the pittas. If you want to save it for later, wrap and chill until ready to eat. It will keep fairly crisp for about 2 hours.

Serves 4

Points per serving 2
Total Points 8
Calories per serving 70

115 g (4 oz) cooked skinless, boneless
    chicken breast
85 g (3 oz) lean ham, de-rinded and cubed
a little freshly ground nutmeg
2 tablespoons low-fat plain fromage frais
1 tablespoon sweet pickle
freshly ground black pepper

Chicken and Bacon Paste

Freezing recommended • Preparation time: 20 minutes + chilling.
This wholesome home-made pâté is excellent in sandwiches, topped
with cress, tomato and cucumber.

1 Put the chicken and ham into a food processor with the nutmeg,
fromage frais, pickle and pepper, to taste. Whizz until it is a chunky
purée or, if you like, make it finer. Alternatively, put the meats through
a mincer twice and then mix with the other ingredients.
2 Spoon into a food container and chill until firm.

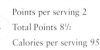

Serves 4

Points per serving 2
Total Points 8½
Calories per serving 95

4 ripe tomatoes, de-seeded and chopped
    into small chunks
½ cucumber, chopped into chunks
¼ iceberg lettuce, shredded coarsely
8 black olives, stoned and sliced
2 tablespoons chopped fresh parsley
100 g (3½ oz) feta cheese
2 tablespoons fat-free dressing of your
    choice or fresh lemon juice
freshly ground black pepper

Greek Salad

Ⓥ if vegetarian cheese is used • Freezing recommended
• Preparation time: 10 minutes. Recapture the sun in your lunch box
with these bright colours and crisp flavours. Although feta is a full-fat,
salty cheese, it is quite strong so you don't need as much.

1 Mix the vegetables, olives and parsley together. Season with pepper
and place in food containers as required.
2 Crumble over the feta, cover and chill until required. If you are not
going to eat it immediately, only toss in the dressing just before eating
so the leaves remain crisp.

Serves **4**

Points per serving 2

Total Points 7½

Calories per serving 140

100 g (3½ oz) bulghur wheat

3 firm tomatoes, skinned and chopped

4 tablespoons fresh lemon juice

1 tablespoon olive oil, preferably
    extra-virgin

4 tablespoons chopped fresh parsley

3 tablespoons chopped fresh mint

2 salad onions, chopped finely

salt and freshly ground black pepper

Tabbouleh

Ⓥ Freezing not recommended • Preparation time: 10 minutes + 20 minutes soaking + 1 hour chilling. Bulghur wheat needs no cooking – you simply cover it with water to soak and plump up. Then mix with finely chopped salad vegetables. The fresh herbs are very much part of the dish but they are easy to buy or you may have an abundance growing in your garden.

1 Put the bulghur wheat in a large bowl and cover with cold water. Stir once, then leave for about 20 minutes to bulk up. Drain, pressing down on it in the colander with the back of a ladle.

2 Meanwhile, score the top of the tomatoes and plunge them into a bowl of boiling water for a minute. Remove, run under cold water and skin. Discard the core, then chop finely.

3 Mix the wheat with all the other ingredients, season well and then chill for at least an hour if possible to allow the flavours to mature.

Menu Plan

Breakfast		Lunch		Dinner	
Medium bowl 30 g (1¼ oz) cornflakes		Greek Salad		Medium pork loin chop	5 Points
	1½ Points	(1 serving) page 127	2 Points	2 tablespoons apple sauce	½ Point
1 tablespoon sultanas	1 Point	Medium pitta	2½ Points	Medium portion 200 g (7 oz) boiled	
¼ pint skimmed milk	½ Points	3 plums	½ Point	potatoes	2 Points
				Carrots, broccoli, cauliflower	0 Points
				Small tub low-fat plain yogurt	
					1½ Points

Throughout the day: ½ pint skimmed milk *1 Point*   **Treat:** 2 scoops low-fat ice cream *2 Points*

Sweet
Things

We all like to treat ourselves to something sweet now and again, and why not? These recipes are ideal for spoiling yourself and your friends or family at tea time or after a meal. As an added bonus, because most of them have fruit, they are good for you too. Fruit is very healthy; in fact you should try to eat five portions of fruit and vegetables a day and that can include canned or frozen fruit. These recipes use low-fat dairy products which are every bit as creamy as those which are high in fat. They also use unrefined sugar which is not lower in Points or Calories but does have a better taste than refined sugar. If you would like to use an artificial sweetener, be sure to add it at the end of the recipe if it is a hot dessert because the taste is affected by high heat.

If you thought that goodies such as chocolate, ice cream, bread and butter pudding were things of the past, think again – with Weight Watchers, you just count the Points and enjoy what you fancy!

Serves 4 | Points per serving 4½
Total Points 17½
Calories per serving 285

Apricot Rice Pudding

125 g (4½ oz) rice e.g. Thai, basmati,
    arborio or pudding
1 litre (1¾ pints) skimmed milk
50 g (1¾ oz) unrefined light soft brown
    sugar, to taste
1 large bay leaf or 1 cinnamon stick
    (optional)
3 tablespoons low-fat fromage frais
400 g (14 oz) canned apricot halves in
    natural juice, drained

Ⓥ Freezing not recommended • Preparation time: 10 minutes + 30 minutes cooking + cooling. A rice pudding made with skimmed milk is a healthy low-fat pudding. It tastes rich though because the starch in the rice gives it a creamy texture. This recipe is best served lightly chilled.

1 Put the rice, milk, brown sugar and bay leaf or cinnamon stick, if using, into a large non-stick saucepan. Bring to the boil slowly, stirring.
2 When the milk is boiling, turn down to a gentle simmer, stirring occasionally until the milk has reduced and the rice has thickened. How long you need to cook it will depend on which rice you use, but generally, allow 20–30 minutes.
3 Remove from the heat and cool. Remove the bay leaf or cinnamon stick, if using. When cold, fold in the fromage frais.
4 Divide the apricots between four sundae glasses and spoon the rice pudding on top. Alternatively, put the rice on the base and the fruit on top.

Weight Watchers note: If you want to make this recipe with artificial sweetener instead of sugar, add it in step 3 after the fromage frais and deduct 1 Point per serving.

Serves 4 | Points per serving 2½
Total Points 10
Calories per serving 160

Sticky Hot Bananas

2 tablespoons unrefined soft light brown
    sugar
1 tablespoon water
2 teaspoons butter-flavour low-fat spread
1 teaspoon lemon juice
4 medium bananas (ripe, with spotty
    skins), peeled and halved lengthways
a little grated lemon zest, to serve
    (optional)

Ⓥ Freezing not recommended • Preparation and cooking time: 10 minutes. Bananas are wonderfully versatile fruits. Here they are sliced and 'pan-fried' in a light syrup and then served with small scoops of Weight Watchers from Heinz Ice Cream or thick low-fat plain yogurt.

1 Put the sugar and water into a frying-pan and heat slowly to dissolve, stirring often. Mix in the low-fat spread and lemon juice. Bring to a simmer.
2 Lower in the banana halves and stir gently to coat them in syrup. Cook for about 2 minutes until they are hot but not soft. Allow to cool slightly before serving. Grate a little lemon zest on top, if you wish.

Apricot Rice Pudding
Iced Coffee Jelly *(page 134)*

Serves 4

Points per serving 4
Total Points 15½
Calories per serving 265

low-fat cooking spray

2 eggs, at room temperature

90 g (3¼ oz) caster sugar

90 g (3¼ oz) plain flour, sifted

For the filling:

150 g (5½ oz) raspberries, thawed if
frozen

200 g (7 oz) skimmed milk soft cheese
e.g. quark

sugar or artificial sweetener, to taste

125 g (4½ oz) fresh strawberries, halved

a few sprigs of mint, to decorate (optional)

Red Berry Flan

Red Berry Flan

Ⓥ if free-range eggs are used • Freezing recommended for the base flan • Preparation time: 25 minutes + 30 minutes baking.

1 Preheat the oven to Gas Mark 3/170°C/325°F. Spray a non-stick 20 cm (8-inch) sponge flan tin with low-fat spray.

2 Place a heatproof mixing bowl on top of a saucepan of water, bring to a boil, and then turn the heat down to bring it to a simmer.

3 Put the eggs and caster sugar into the bowl and using an electric hand whisk, beat together until you have a pale golden, thick foam. To check for the right consistency, lift up the beaters and let a trail of foam fall back into the bowl; it should hold its shape well without dissolving.

4 Remove the bowl from the heat and continue whisking the foam for another 2 minutes to cool it down slightly.

5 Sprinkle some flour around the sides of the bowl and, using a large metal spoon, carefully fold in the flour using a gentle figure of eight motion. If a few flecks of flour remain, don't worry. Scoop carefully into the prepared tin and level off the top.

6 Bake for about 25–30 minutes or until the top feels firm and springy to the touch. Remove from the oven and cool for 5 minutes, then turn out on to a wire rack to cool.

7 Now make the filling. Crush the raspberries with a fork but not to a purée consistency. (Thawed raspberries will not need much crushing.) Beat the soft cheese separately with a wooden spoon until smooth and then add sugar or sweetener, to taste, before folding in the raspberries.

8 Spoon the filling into the cooled flan in spoonfuls in such a way that the mixture looks light and inviting. Decorate the flan with the strawberry halves and sprigs of mint leaves, if using.

Menu Plan

Breakfast	Lunch	Dinner
½ medium Galia melon 250 g (9 oz) *1 Point*	Small can 300 g (10½ oz) Chicken & Vegetable or Vegetable soup *1½ Points*	Lean medium gammon steak 175 g (6 oz) cooked *5 Points*
Medium bowl 30 g (1¼ oz) Ready Brek *1½ Points*	Carrot & celery sticks, yellow, green & red pepper strips, broccoli florets *0 Points*	Pineapple ring *0 Points*
Granulated artificial sweetener if desired *0 Points*	2 tablespoons guacamole or hummous *3 Points*	200 g (7 oz) boiled potatoes *2 Points*
		Green beans, Brussels sprouts *0 Points*
		Sticky Hot Bananas (1 serving) page 130 *2½ Points*

Throughout the day: 1 pint skimmed milk *2 Points*   **Treat:** Small packet fruit pastilles *1½ Points*

Cranberry and Orange Jellies

2 sachets of gelatine crystals

600 ml (1 pint) cranberry juice (without sugar)

600 ml (1 pint) orange juice (preferably freshly squeezed with 'bits')

2 tablespoons clear honey

4 tablespoons low-fat plain yogurt, to serve

**Freezing not recommended • Preparation time: 15 minutes +
setting.** This is a quick and easy pudding that is fun to make and fun
to serve. You will need 4 sundae or tall wine glasses.

1 Put 3 tablespoons of cold water into a small saucepan and stir in the
gelatine crystals. Leave to 'sponge' (that is, 'go solid'), then over a very
low heat melt gently, without stirring, until all the grains have
dissolved. Then stir very gently to blend.

2 Divide the dissolved gelatine equally between two jugs. Quickly add
the cranberry juice to one jug, and the orange juice to the other. Add 1
tablespoon of honey to each juice.

3 Now for the fun part! Divide half of the cranberry mixture between
two sundae glasses or tall wine glasses and then put half of the orange
mixture into another two sundae glasses or tall wine glasses. Leave all
four glasses to set in the fridge but leave the remaining juice in the jugs
at room temperature so that they don't set.

4 When the jellies in the glasses have set, pour the juices from the jugs
on top, putting the cranberry mixture on top of the orange jelly and the
orange mixture on top of the cranberry jelly. Return to the fridge to set.

5 Serve the jellies with a thin layer of low-fat plain yogurt on top.

Iced Coffee Jelly

600 ml (1 pint) skimmed milk

**2 tablespoons instant coffee granules
(choose good quality for best flavour)**

a good pinch of ground cinnamon

**50 g (1¾ oz) unrefined light muscovado
sugar or light soft brown sugar**

1 sachet of gelatine crystals

To serve:

2 medium bananas

**1 small square of dark chocolate, grated
finely**

**Freezing not recommended • Preparation time: 10 minutes +
setting time.** Cool and refreshing – yet another way to enjoy the
delicious flavour of coffee.

1 Put the milk into a saucepan and bring to the boil. When it starts to
rise up the pan, whisk in the coffee, cinnamon and sugar. Stir well until
dissolved.

2 Remove the pan from the heat and immediately whisk in the
gelatine crystals, stirring for a good minute until all the crystals have
dissolved. Leave to cool, stirring occasionally to stop a skin forming.

3 Wet a jelly mould with cold water and pour in the cooled mixture or
simply pour it straight into a pretty serving dish. Chill until set and if it
is in a mould, turn out by briefly dipping the mould into very hot
water.

4 If you wish, serve with sliced bananas and a very light sprinkling of
finely grated chocolate.

Serves **4**

Points per serving 2½
Total Points 9
Calories per serving 150

Apple Crackers

4 Granny Smith apples, peeled and chopped into small chunks
1 tablespoon caster sugar
½ teaspoon cinnamon or mixed spice or 4 whole cloves
low-fat cooking spray (optional)
4 teaspoons low-fat spread, melted
4 sheets of filo pastry
a little icing sugar, for dusting

ⓥ Freezing recommended at the end of step 4, before cooking
● Preparation time: 20 minutes + cooling + 20–25 minutes baking.
The easiest apple turnovers ever!

1 Place the apple chunks in a saucepan with the sugar, spice of your choice and 2 tablespoons of water.

2 Bring to the boil, then cover and cook gently for 5 minutes until softened but still holding a good shape. Check for sweetness adding more sugar if required. Set aside to cool thoroughly.

3 Preheat the oven to Gas Mark 5/190°C/375°F. Spray a baking sheet with low-fat cooking spray, if using.

4 Melt the low-fat spread in a cup and add 1 tablespoon of water. Take a sheet of filo, brush it lightly with the fat and water mixture, then fold in half widthways. Spoon a quarter of the apple filling at the top edge along the widest side and roll loosely up. Press the ends together lightly like a cracker.

5 Place the cracker on the baking sheet and repeat the process in step 4 with the other sheets and remaining filling. If you have any fat and water mixture left, then brush this on top of the crackers. Bake for about 20–25 minutes until golden brown and crisp. Remove to a wire rack to cool and serve warm dusted with icing sugar.

Menu Plan

Breakfast		Lunch		Dinner	
½ medium Galia melon 250 g (9 oz)		2 medium slices bread	2 Points	6 pieces chicken nuggets	4½ Points
	1 Point	2 medium turkey rashers	1 Point	Small portion 100 g (3½ oz) thick-cut	
Small slice malt loaf	1½ Points	2 teaspoons tomato ketchup or brown		oven-baked chips	3 Points
1 teaspoon low-fat spread	½ Point	sauce	0 Points	Mushrooms, tomatoes	0 Points
		small tub low-fat plain yogurt		**Iced Coffee Jelly**	
			1½ Points	(1 serving), opposite	2 Points
		Small banana	1 Point		

Throughout the day: ½ pint skimmed milk *1 Point*   **Treat:** Small bunch 100 g (3½ oz) grapes *1 Point*

500 g (1 lb 2 oz) bio-yogurt

2 tablespoons clear honey

some artificial sweetener (optional)

2 tablespoons unrefined demerara sugar

400 g (14 oz) canned peach slices in
    natural juice, drained

½ teaspoon ground mixed spice or ground
    cinnamon

grated zest of 1 small orange or lemon

Spiced Peaches with Honeyed Yogurt

Ⓥ Freezing not recommended • Preparation time: 10 minutes + 1 hour chilling. A quick and easy pudding with the taste of summer. Serve with a low-fat rich tea biscuit and remember to add the extra Points.

1 Beat the yogurt with clear honey and taste for sweetness. Add some artificial sweetener if you wish, keeping in mind that more sugar will go on top. Put the yogurt into a serving dish and sprinkle over 1 tablespoon of demerara. Chill for at least an hour.

2 Put the peach slices into a saucepan with the remaining demerara sugar and the spice. Heat gently but do not allow to boil. Serve alongside the chilled honey yogurt. Decorate with the grated zest.

1 packet of sugar-free lemon jelly

grated zest and juice of 1 lemon (optional)

200 g (7 oz) very-low-fat fromage frais e.g.
    strawberry or exotic fruits

2 egg whites

Lemony Mousse

Freezing not recommended • Preparation time: 10 minutes + chilling and setting. Light, luscious and lemony – a wonderful way to end a meal.

1 Dissolve the lemon jelly in 200 ml (7 fl oz) boiling water. For an extra-lemony flavour, add the lemon zest and juice. Leave to cool.

2 Blend well with the fromage frais and put the bowl in the fridge to start to set. This may take about 3 hours or so, depending on the outside temperature.

3 When the edges of the mixture look wobbly and are starting to set, whisk the egg whites briskly until they are a light, frothy foam with soft floppy peaks. Using a large metal spoon, gently fold the egg whites into the setting mixture using a figure of eight motion.

4 Pour into four pretty wine glasses or a large glass bowl. Leave until set. When it is ready, it will be soft and creamy.

Spiced Peaches with Honeyed Yogurt
Baby Bread and Butter Pud *(page 142)*

Fruit 'Kebabs' with Chocolate Dipping Sauce

50 g (1¾ oz) dark plain chocolate (with at least 50% cocoa solids)

1 tablespoon clear honey

grated zest and juice of 1 small orange (optional)

2 medium bananas, cut into bite-size chunks

250 g (9 oz) fresh strawberries

4 wooden satay sticks

Ⓥ **Freezing not recommended • Preparation time: 15 minutes + cooling.** Watch a small bar of chocolate stretch to feed four!

1 Break the chocolate into squares and put them either in a small saucepan (if using the stove) or a microwave-proof bowl. Add 5 tablespoons of water, the honey and orange zest.

2 Melt the chocolate either over a very low heat in the pan, stirring frequently, or put the uncovered bowl on full power in a microwave for a minute. Stir and heat again. Heat the chocolate until it has all melted and is smooth. Do not let the mixture bubble or it will 'seize'.

3 Cool, stirring often to stop a skin forming, until thickened. When cooled to room temperature, pour into a small and pretty serving bowl.

4 Toss the bananas in the orange juice, if using. Spear the strawberries and banana chunks on to the satay sticks.

5 Arrange the fruit kebabs around the dipping sauce and serve.

Pear and Ice Cream Melba

400 g (14 oz) canned pear quarters in natural juice, drained

4 x 60 g (2¼ oz) scoops of Weight Watchers from Heinz ice cream (any flavour)

For the sauce:

250 g (9 oz) fresh raspberries

1 tablespoon icing sugar

2 teaspoons fresh lemon juice

Ⓥ **Freezing recommended • Preparation time: 10 minutes.**
It's hard to improve on ice cream – but pears and a raspberry sauce make it taste sublime.

1 To make the sauce, whizz the raspberries in a food processor or blender with the icing sugar and lemon juice. When the consistency is runny, pass it through a large sieve, rubbing with the back of a wooden spoon, if necessary.

2 Place the pears in four sundae dishes. Top with scoops of ice cream and drizzle the sauce on top.

Variation: Sprinkle with some chopped toasted hazelnuts or almonds and add a ½ Point per serving.

Fruit 'Kebabs' with Chocolate Dipping Sauce

2 large oranges

2 sweet grapefruit

300 ml (10 fl oz) apple juice

1 sachet of gelatine crystals

whole mint leaves for the base (optional)

250 g (9 oz) firm strawberries (large ones
    cut in half)

1 tablespoon clear honey or artificial
    sweetener, to taste (optional)

Citrus Fruit and Strawberry Terrine

Freezing not recommended • **Preparation time: 40 minutes +
chilling.** A pretty and refreshingly tangy dessert.

1 Grate the zest from one orange and one grapefruit. Cut the peel
from both the oranges and both the grapefruit making sure you also
remove the white pith. Catch any juice which may be squeezed out in a
bowl and save it. Slice the oranges and grapefruit thinly and cut them
into half moons.

2 Line the base of a 500 g (1 lb 2 oz) loaf tin with a sheet of baking
parchment.

3 Heat the apple juice with any saved juices from the oranges and
grapefruit with the two zests until boiling. Then remove from the heat
and sprinkle over the gelatine, whisking until dissolved. If using, add
either the honey or artificial sweetener, to taste. Set aside to cool.

4 Pour a very thin layer of cooled juice on the base of the tin and
leave to set in the fridge. Lay mint leaves on top and then place
alternating slices of orange and grapefruit on top.

5 Layer the strawberries randomly, keeping in mind how the
terrine will look once it has been turned out. (The base will, obviously,
be the top.)

6 Slowly pour the remaining juice over the fruits, tapping the tin
gently to get rid of air bubbles. Chill in the fridge until really firm.

7 To turn out, fill a basin with very hot water and hold the tin in it to
the count of 5. Run a table knife around the inside and shake out on to
a slightly wet serving plate. (This is so you can move the terrine if it
falls off centre.) If the terrine doesn't come out, dip it in hot water and
shake again until it does. Peel off the paper carefully. Cut in slices with
a serrated knife and lift onto serving plates with a fish slice or pie
server.

Weight Watchers note: If the optional honey is used, add an extra ½
Point per serving.

Citrus Fruit and Strawberry Terrine

Pear and Ice Cream Melba *(page 139)*

Serves **4** | Points per serving 4½
Total Points 17½
Calories per serving 275

Baby Bread and Butter Puds

6 medium slices of white bread, crusts removed

4 teaspoons low-fat spread

low-fat cooking spray

1 tablespoon mixed peel (optional)

50 g (1½ oz) sultanas or raisins

grated zest of 1 lemon or 1 small orange

500 ml (18 fl oz) skimmed milk

3 tablespoons unrefined soft brown sugar

2 eggs

Ⓥ if free-range eggs are used • Freezing not recommended • Preparation time: 25 minutes + 30 minutes standing + 20–30 minutes baking. The secret to a light bread and butter pudding is to let the mixture soak into the bread before baking.

1 Using scone cutters, cut twelve discs out of the bread just to fit inside 4 medium-size ramekins. Spread the bread lightly with the low-fat spread.

2 Spray the insides of the ramekins with the cooking spray. Mix the peel, if using, with the sultanas and the grated zest. Place a bread disc in the bottom of each ramekin, divide the fruit mixture evenly among the ramekins, repeat and top with a bread disc with the low-fat spread side facing up.

3 Bring the milk to the boil with the soft brown sugar, stirring until dissolved. Remove and cool for 5 minutes.

4 Meanwhile, beat the eggs in a heatproof bowl. Add the sweet milk to the eggs and beat well. Slowly pour the mixture over the filled ramekins and down the insides.

5 Leave for about half an hour to allow the liquid to sink into the bread. Preheat the oven to Gas Mark 5/190°C/375°F. Stand the ramekins in a small roasting pan filled with hot water which comes two-thirds of the way up the dishes.

6 Bake for about 20–30 minutes or until risen and golden and crisp on top. Stand for 5 minutes before serving.

Variation: Try using different types of bread in this pudding: stale French bread or even a thinly sliced malt loaf would work well.

Weight Watchers note: If you wish, you can sprinkle each pud with a teaspoon of demera sugar. Add a ½ Point per serving.

Index